How to Live *for* God *in a* Hostile World

John Robert Bracamontes

How to Live for God in a Hostile World

Life Applications of 1 Peter

TATE PUBLISHING
AND ENTERPRISES, LLC

How to Live for God in a Hostile World
Copyright © 2015 by John Robert Bracamontes. All rights reserved.

No part of this publication may be reproduced, stored in a retrieval system or transmitted in any way by any means, electronic, mechanical, photocopy, recording or otherwise without the prior permission of the author except as provided by USA copyright law.

Scripture quotations marked (NIV) are taken from the *Holy Bible, New International Version*®, NIV®. Copyright © 1973, 1978, 1984, 2011 by Biblica, Inc.™ Used by permission of Zondervan. All rights reserved worldwide. www.zondervan.com

Scripture quotations marked (NKJV) are taken from the *New King James Version*®. Copyright © 1982 by Thomas Nelson, Inc. Used by permission. All rights reserved.

This book is designed to provide accurate and authoritative information with regard to the subject matter covered. This information is given with the understanding that neither the author nor Tate Publishing, LLC is engaged in rendering legal, professional advice. Since the details of your situation are fact dependent, you should additionally seek the services of a competent professional.

The opinions expressed by the author are not necessarily those of Tate Publishing, LLC.

Published by Tate Publishing & Enterprises, LLC
127 E. Trade Center Terrace | Mustang, Oklahoma 73064 USA
1.888.361.9473 | www.tatepublishing.com

Tate Publishing is committed to excellence in the publishing industry. The company reflects the philosophy established by the founders, based on Psalm 68:11,
"The Lord gave the word and great was the company of those who published it."

Book design copyright © 2015 by Tate Publishing, LLC. All rights reserved.
Cover design by Jeffrey Doblados
Interior design by Mary Jean Archival

Published in the United States of America

ISBN: 978-1-63449-113-6
1. Religion / Christian Life / Spiritual Growth
2. Religion / Biblical Studies / New Testament
15.02.06

Contents

Preface 9
Introduction 11
Chapter 1 15
  Introduction and Greeting to the Churches 15
    What's in a Name? 15
    Ministry Authority 17
    We Are God's Chosen People 18
  Salvation through the New Birth and Our Joyful,
  Empowered Response 20
    New Birth and Mercy 20
    Birthed into a Living Hope through the
    Resurrection 21
    Birthed into an Inheritance: Imperishable,
    Undefiled, and Unfading 22
    Birthed into a Salvation Ready to Be Revealed 23

Rejoice for the Future while Enduring
    Testing Now 25
Love, Believe, Rejoice.. 26
The Prophecies Are for Us 28
Practical Response to Our Glorious Salvation 29
The Call to Holy Living... 31
Living in Godly Reverence in View of God's
    Judgment and Redemption 35
    Life of Reverence 36
    Redeemed by Christ's Sacrifice................................. 36
    Redemption Planned Before Creation 37
Obedient Purifying Love and New Birth
    through the Word of God................................... 38
    Consecration to the Lord through Loving the
        Christian Family.. 38
    The Word of God Brings New Birth 41

Chapter 2 43
Put Away Vices and Crave the Spiritual
    Nourishment of the Lord 43
    Vicious Vices 43
    Crave Pure Spiritual Milk and Grow..................... 45
Christ Is the Living Stone upon which the
    Church Is Founded... 47
Christ the Cornerstone in Whom We Trust 50
Jesus—Precious to Believers but a Rocky Road
    for Unbelievers.. 52
God's Chosen People 54
How to Live Out the Principles of God's
    Kingdom.. 57

  Responsibilities in the Home and Church................57
  Civil Responsibilities 60
 Submission of Slaves to Masters: How Is This
  Relevant for Today? 65
 To This You Were Called 67

Chapter 3 75
 The Relationship of Wives to Husbands and
  Their Witness 75
 The Relationship of Husbands to Wives 81
 Directions for Everyone 83
 What If You Suffer for Doing Good? 90
 Christ's Sufferings: Why Unjust Suffering Is to
  Be Endured 94

Chapter 4 99
 Victory Over the Sinful Nature 99
 Obedience to Christ: Our Way of Life 101
 The End Is Near: Love and Serve One Another.....105
  Specific Ways to Live Out Love 108
 Rejoice in Suffering and Commit Yourself to
  God 109
 Suffer for Christ, Not for Personal Crimes or
  Offenses 112

Chapter 5 117
 Peter Gives Words of Wisdom to Church
  Leaders 117
  Peter: A Fellow Elder and Governance of the
   Church 117
 Pastoral Responsibilities.. 120

Pastoral Reward 122
Responsibilities of the Church: Humility, Trust,
   and Self-Control... 123
Victory Over the Enemy of Our Souls 127
The Stabilizing Grace of God 130
Final Greetings 131

Bibliography 135

Preface

This work was born out of my own personal study and meditation. Having spent countless hours memorizing it and meditating on it, 1 Peter has been one of my favorite books of the Bible to read and study. My reading and study of 1 Peter, using the Greek text, is what finally resulted in this writing. Each word was analyzed according to its grammatical part of speech and lexical meaning, studying each phrase and clause, understanding its grammatical function within each sentence. After this, a structural outline of the Greek text was made. It was from this outline that each verse was translated, analyzed, and applied. I have included a modified translation of the American Standard Version based on exegetical study of the Greek text.

The main body of this work is not intended to be a technical reference but rather an inspirational application commentary for the church. We recognize that although

Peter's epistle was not written to us directly, it was written for our benefit as well. Though we live in a different time and culture, the principles of faith learned from these exhortations help us give modern-day biblical expression to our relationship with God and fellow humanity.

Introduction

Every Christian is faced with the challenges of life that can result in a personal identity crisis. As we come to terms with who Jesus is in our lives, we are also faced with the question of who we are in Christ. Understanding this becomes the key for how Christians can live for God in this hostile world.

This book surveys the life-changing message of 1 Peter, showing how personal identity is built upon a saving relationship with God as Father, with Jesus Christ as savior and coming deliverer, and with the Holy Spirit who purifies our hearts and gives us Christ's resurrected life. The hope-filled message of 1 Peter continually points the Christian to the victorious return of Jesus Christ that will bring the final victory for each child of God. Having this eternal hope brings great strength and endurance to walk the Christian life in fellowship with both God and the Christian family found in the church. As each of us battles with the world, the flesh, and the devil, none of us is alone. The spiritual and personal connections God provides for us are stronger than the struggles we face. We can find comfort and strength in God's personal presence, the hope of his life-giving return, and Christian fellowship in the church. We are God's chosen people.

The apostle Peter was fulfilling the ministry to which Jesus had appointed him by writing this letter to the saints. We remember the exhortation our Lord spoke to him, "Feed my sheep" (John 21:16–17). While Peter addressed a group of believers in a particular geographical setting at a particular time in history other than our own, his words reverberate throughout the world, even to us in this day and age. He spoke of our great salvation, of the new birth we have received, and of a practical response to the new birth that commands our obedience and solicits our love both to him and our Christian family.

Peter did not refer to himself very often. In fact, there are only three references. First, he identified himself as an apostle of Jesus Christ. Second, he mentioned himself as a fellow elder among elders and a witness of Christ's sufferings, one who will share in future glory. Finally, he mentioned that he obtained help from Silas in the writing of his letter. Peter was aware of his own apostolic calling and authority, yet he maintained a humble spirit when he identified himself as a *fellow* elder. He was one who gave credit where credit was due when he acknowledged the help of Silas.

His audience was not a single church but many churches, which he called "God's elect" and "strangers in the world," that were geographically scattered throughout Pontus, Galatia, Cappadocia, Asia, and Bithynia. These include regions where Paul the apostle evangelized during his early missionary work. Peter primarily addressed gentiles within these regions, although there was the likelihood that there were Jewish Christians present as well. However, his reference to their former "empty way of life handed down to you from your forefathers" (1 Peter 1:8) suggests a gentile audience converted from paganism. The Jewish faith would not have been an empty way of life. Furthermore, they had "spent enough time in the past doing what pagans choose to do—living in debauchery, lust, drunkenness, orgies, carousing, and detestable idolatry." He was not referring simply to an individual living in this manner but an entire group of people following these ways. This would have certainly characterized the Greco-Roman way of life, not Judaism.

Furthermore, his audience was not the lost but rather gentiles who had accepted the faith and forsook their old way of life. While Peter was addressing everyone in the church and giving general exhortations that apply to all, he did single out specific groups in the church, addressing the family unit, specifically speaking to husbands and wives and household slaves. Near the end of his letter, he addressed the church leadership, giving encouragement to the elders and calling the young men to honor their more elder leadership.

As we read Peter's writings, we seek first to understand what he wrote to these churches, what he intended to communicate to them. We then look to apply these principles to our own lives so that we can live God's truth practically. Practical living of these truths will be worked out within both our divine and human relationships, with both God and man.

Chapter 1

Introduction and Greeting to the Churches

> Peter, an apostle of Jesus Christ, to chosen sojourners scattered throughout Pontus, Galatia, Cappadocia, Asia, and Bithynia, chosen according to the foreknowledge of God the Father, through sanctification by the Spirit, for the purpose of obedience and sprinkling with the blood of Jesus Christ: Grace and peace be multiplied to you.
>
> —1 Peter 1:1–2

What's in a Name?

Peter identified himself by the name Jesus gave him—Rock, which came from the Greek *petros*. Christ has an identity for each of us, a new way of seeing ourselves in relationship with him, indicating a new way of life.

When I named my children, I named them with specific meanings in mind to reflect something of the nature of God. God has a name and identity for each of us. The book of Revelation shows God giving each of us a secret name that is between us and him.

> He who has an ear, let him hear what the Spirit says to the churches. To him who overcomes I will give some of the hidden manna to eat. And I will give him a white stone, and on the stone a new name written which no one knows except him who receives it. (Revelation 2:17, NKJV)

In both the Hebrew Scriptures and New Testament, we see God naming or changing the names of his servants: Adam, Abraham, Sarah, Israel, John the Baptist, Jesus, Peter. Especially in Biblical times, names carried great meaning, conveying something of one's identity. As an apostle of Jesus Christ, not only was Simon Peter given a new name, he was also given a ministry, a change of vocation. Most of us will not be called to a new vocation, but we are called to ministry and service and a new way of life. Some of you will be called to vocational ministry that will require abandoning the nets and boats by the shore (like the apostles), finding your income through ministry and service to God. What is your ministry? How will you find it? Follow the known and revealed will of God found in the Scriptures. If there is more for you to do, he will show it to you.

Ministry Authority

Peter appealed to the authority he had received from Christ. In addition to the call of ministry, he received the authority to carry it out. Occasions may come when we must appeal to the authority God has given to us as we execute our service to God. Paul on occasion did the same thing. This must be done with gentleness and respect, without pomp or condescension, but in humility and grace.

The apostolic authority of this epistle extends to us, even today. As we read the words of Scripture, we can acknowledge the authority of God's Word over our lives. Peter's apostolic authority was derived from Christ, and, therefore, the message bears the authority of Christ himself. Remember, "If anyone speaks, let him speak as if he were speaking the very words of God" (1 Peter 4:11). Should we approach this epistle or any other writing of Scripture as anything less?

Not only do we acknowledge that Peter had authority as an apostle, but all those he called into service have authority from God. We do not all have the same level of authority, but we all have been given responsibility and Christ's authority to execute our duties. By choosing to submit to church authority, beginning with the apostolic authority of the Bible, we are submitting to God and opening the channel for serving God with his stamp of approval. Can you think of areas in your life where you can improve your spiritual submission and where you can assert the responsibilities of your call with the authority of Christ? Remember, this is to be done with all humility.

We Are God's Chosen People

Peter addressed the recipients of his letter in a way that identified them as the chosen people of God, specifically chosen sojourners (wanderers or travelers) of the diaspora or scattering. Diaspora means scattering and specifically refers to Israel when they were scattered throughout the then known world during captivity. More generally, the idea has been used to refer to all God's people who are scattered all over the world. This has been a designation for the people of God, beginning with the election of Abraham, who was called to leave his homeland and go to a place that God would show him. He was one of the many nomadic immigrants from his country but the only man of faith through whom God would raise a family.

The Church continues to be a people who are passing through and who look forward to the city whose builder and maker is God. We are in the world, but for sure we are not of it. This parallels the work of Paul in Ephesians, which states that there is one people of God, not two separate groups—Jewish Christian and Gentile Christian. There is no spiritual apartheid in God's kingdom. This perspective of "just passing through" is necessary and liberating—necessary that we may keep our eternal inheritance in mind, and liberating in that it frees us to abandon the things of this life that attempt to keep us from our journey of faith.

They were the chosen (as are we) by a threefold work of God in the persons of the Father, the Holy Spirit, and the Son Jesus Christ. First, according to the foreknowledge of God the Father, he knew the plan. Second, by the sanctifying work of the Spirit, he prepares us for the plan. Third, this choosing by the sanctifying work of the Spirit is to result in obedience and purification from sin, a sprinkling by the blood of Jesus Christ (Old Testament imagery of sacrifice and atonement). Jesus administers the plan of salvation by his blood.

Finally, after identifying who these Christians were, he spoke of a blessing of multiplied and abundant grace and peace—the grace that embodies all the blessings of God, and the peace that comes from God. Not only do we have a peace that comes from God but also peace with God that surpasses our understanding and preserves us and makes us whole. This "wholeness" is described by the Hebrew word *shalom*, much more than personal peace, but soundness of being.

Peter's introduction addresses the question to whom this letter was written, but even more, who Christians are in Christ. How do we apply these truths to our own lives? We must see ourselves as God sees us and call ourselves as God has called us. We are his precious people, though in this world we are not of it, his servants who are sent to a lost and dying world. Even though this is merely Peter's introduction to his letter, it is nevertheless very much a spiritual exhortation, describing who we are in our relationship to God and describing our great blessings.

Salvation through the New Birth and Our Joyful, Empowered Response

> Blessed is the God and Father of our Lord Jesus Christ. According to his great mercy he has given us birth into a living hope by the resurrection of Jesus Christ from the dead, and into an imperishable and undefiled inheritance, beyond the reach of decay, that does not fade away. This inheritance has been kept in heaven for you, who by the power of God are guarded through faith resulting in a salvation ready to be revealed in the last time.
>
> —1 Peter 1:3–5

New Birth and Mercy

Peter turns our attention to our blessed God and Father who deserves exaltation and eternal praise for what he has done, giving us a new birth. We have experienced this great event, and as we learn more about this birth and the benefits proceeding from being God's children, we will rejoice even more and exult in God our Savior. Our lives have been changed for eternity now that we are children of God.

He has given us new birth. We are God's children, sons and daughters of the living God. We have been born anew into the kingdom of God, given the full rights of family members offered to all those who will reverence him and honor him with faith. On account of his awesome love, he has given us life, making us alive with Christ through the resurrection. This new birth brought us out of the death caused by sin. We have been saved by his grace. God has raised us up with Christ and seated us in heaven, commissioning us with his own authority.

The Hebrew Scriptures introduce the concept of God's love in terms of covenant mercy. The Hebrew word correlating to New Testament mercy is *hesed*.[1] While *hesed* is often used with human relationships in the Bible, it also describes the mercy of God that is closely associated with salvation and his covenant. It is through this covenant mercy that we are born again through the covenant of redemption in the blood of Christ.

Birthed into a Living Hope through the Resurrection

Our Father God has birthed us into his living hope, a hope that leads to life and makes us truly alive. Hope is something oriented to the future, not something presently obtained. Who hopes for something he or she already has? Yet, this future hope gives us stability and direction in the here and now. Ultimately, this living hope is our future resurrection. Yet, we are even now raised with Christ in newness of life, a spiritual resurrection. However, we are also waiting for the future resurrection of our bodies, which will then be transformed into eternal incorruptible bodies. Then we will receive the final consummation of our hope. Are you ready?

---

1. The Greek word for mercy in the NT also occurs in the Greek translation of the OT (called the Septuagint). The Hebrew word translated by the Greek *"eleos" (mercy)* is *"hesed."*

In death, we will not be like those outside of Christ who have no hope. This hope of eternal life is the foundation upon which our faith and knowledge of the truth rests (Titus 1:2). While we live in this age, doing the will of God, we actively await the blessed hope, which is the appearing of our Lord Jesus Christ. At that time, we shall receive our resurrection. Christ himself is this hope. We are in fellowship with Christ even now, but then we shall see him face to face and shall be with him in his glorious resurrection. Jesus is both the resurrection and the life. It all will be given to us through him. Resurrection declared his sonship, and it will also declare ours. Jesus raised Lazarus from a decaying death in miraculous measure, and yet Lazarus died again. We will rise at the word of Christ, nevermore to die, but to live in the eternal glory of our Father God.

Birthed into an Inheritance: Imperishable, Undefiled, and Unfading

As children of God, we are also his heirs. This new birth ushers us into an inheritance that is eternal, which will not decay or rust or wear out from use or age. This inheritance has been kept in heaven for us, guarded, protected, and preserved. Again, Peter emphasizes the future aspect of the benefit of our new birth. There are aspects of our salvation received in the here and now and aspects that are future. The churches are here reminded that they still have much to look forward to. Our present sufferings cannot be compared to the surpassing greatness of the inheritance that awaits us as children of the Living

God. The Holy Spirit himself is a deposit into our lives, guaranteeing the reception of our inheritance until our final redemption at Christ's coming. Jesus himself is the one who mediates and administrates the new covenant of our redemption so that we may receive this eternal inheritance promised to us by our heavenly Father.

As we await the fulfillment of this promised inheritance, we are being protected by God's power through faith. Faith is more than a force of belief; it is a relationship of trust with God. It is part of the armor of defense he has given to us—the shield of faith with which we quench and extinguish all the fiery arrows of the devil. It is through faith that we can endure and stand against the evil days that may come our way.

Birthed into a Salvation Ready to Be Revealed

Not only have we been birthed into a living hope and an inheritance, we have also been birthed into salvation. Once again, the future aspect of our salvation is here in view (1 Peter 1:5), a salvation that is ready to be revealed at the end of days, when Christ returns. Our salvation is both now in our experience of redemption and also yet to come at the resurrection. We have much to look forward to, and we must look forward to it in faith, that we may receive it. Peter was aware of the sufferings these churches were experiencing, and he encouraged them to look forward to all the blessings God had for them.

This salvation is also ours to look forward to. We also are among those to whom the angels are ministering—

we who will inherit salvation (Hebrews 1:14). We will rejoice in that day, when our salvation is revealed. Hope for the future is extended to us. The phrases "about to be revealed" and "last time" both indicate a future salvation, and it is a blessed one at that. Having these future blessings in mind prepares us to endure the trials that are at hand or that may be coming. Yet, in the middle of these challenges of life we have great victory and joy. What are the trials you are experiencing? Can you imagine the joy you will have at the coming of Christ and your trial only a memory? Take time to practice this exercise of imaginative meditation by focusing on the soon coming of Christ.

Peter shows us how to endure the day by following the example of Jesus. We are also reminded of Paul's words: "For the joy set before him he endured…" This is a great principle of life for us because suffering and trials will come, to some more than others, but we will all experience the tribulation of life circumstance. And yet, Christ is our example of endurance leading to a glorious resurrection. Jesus reminded us that in this world we shall have tribulation but to still be of good cheer because he has overcome the world.

The ability to look forward to our future hope, inheritance, and salvation will make us rock solid and unmovable from our firm footing of faith. Our salvation is ready, no more needs to be done, for the work of Christ is complete, but we are waiting for its full manifestation. Salvation will be fully revealed to us in the last day, the day when we shall all be resurrected into our eternal inheritance.

Rejoice for the Future while Enduring Testing Now

> In which [salvation] you rejoice, though now for a little while, if need be, you have experienced grief in various trials, so that the testing of your faith, which is more precious than gold that perishes though it is tested by fire, may be found to result in praise and glory and honor at the revelation of Jesus Christ.
>
> —1 Peter 1:6–7

We can rejoice in our salvation, even though there may be present grief through various trials and tests, which persist for a little while. Our hope of a complete salvation enables us to endure. This truth highlights the importance of having an idea of what this glorious future will be like. The churches Peter addressed are reminded of the great joy of salvation that is theirs and the greatness of that which is to come. However, for a little while, it may have been necessary for them to experience grief through many kinds of life challenges.

The result of this testing of their faith (and ours) is praise, glory, and honor when Jesus is revealed in his coming. This is why the testing of our faith is described as being of much greater value than gold. Having a tested and proven faith is described as more precious than gold, even gold that was refined and tested and purified by fire. Even this pure gold is considered as perishing when compared to our eternal salvation. Such an analogy shows the value and durability of a tested and proven faith. Our temporary experience of grief is in contrast with the long-lasting value of a faith that will result in enduring unmerited gifts from God. Our Father desires to give us praise and glory and honor when Jesus comes in his glory. Jesus himself has said we will shine in glory.

> The Son of Man will send out His angels, and they will gather out of His kingdom all things that offend, and those who practice lawlessness, and will cast them into the furnace of fire. There will be wailing and gnashing of teeth. Then the righteous will shine forth as the sun in the kingdom of their Father. He who has ears to hear, let him hear! (Matthew 13:41–43, NKJV)

In that long awaited for day, we shall be clothed with the praise, glory, and honor that he has reserved for his children. While it is true that God will glorify us and make us shine like the blazing sun in his kingdom, let us focus on giving glory to our Father. He shall glorify us, and we shall glorify him. All this will take place when Christ returns, for whom we yet await.

Love, Believe, Rejoice

> You love him though you have not seen him.
> You believe in him though you do not see
> him now, and you rejoice with an unspeakable
> and glorious joy as you receive the fulfillment
> of your faith, the salvation of your souls.
>
> —1 Peter 1:8–9

Since we are waiting for Jesus to be revealed, we acknowledge that we do not see him at present. If fact, we have never seen him, yet we are able to love him with a sincere spiritual love. Though we have not seen him, we know him as a blind man would know those whom he loves. We have never touched his body, but we have been touched by his Spirit. We are united with him in spirit and will one day be united with him in completeness, seeing him in all his glory. And even though we do not see him now, we are able to have faith in him. He grants us saving faith so that we may know him in the here and now and know him fully and unhidden in the age to come. We also presently rejoice with a joy that is beyond our ability to verbally articulate and a joy that is glorious. It is unspeakable and beyond adequate description being an exalted and glorified joy and a gift from heaven.

The reason for our rejoicing is that we are receiving the end goal of our faith, the salvation of our souls. Love, faith, and rejoicing are emphasized in these two verses with the pronouncement of our salvation. How else can we respond? How can we not love and rejoice and believe? This may be overly simplified but not by much! In spite of any suffering and discomfort of grief, we have every reason for love, faith, and rejoicing. We are currently rejoicing because we are in the process of receiving this great salvation. The time of our rejoicing is now. We have not yet received the fullness that awaits us, and yet we are being filled and are receiving now in part what will be fulfilled in Christ's coming.

The Prophecies Are for Us

> The prophets, who prophesied about the grace given to you, searched diligently and investigated this salvation, inquiring into the details when these things might happen. The Spirit of Christ in them was declaring the sufferings of Christ and the glories to follow his sufferings. It was revealed to them that they were not ministering these things to themselves, but to you. These things have been announced to you through those who preached the gospel to you, by the Holy Spirit sent forth from heaven; things the angels desire to look into.
>
> 1 Peter 1:10–12

The value of this salvation is magnified by the observation that both the prophets who declared this salvation and the angels who observe it are extremely interested in it. The prophets who, by the Holy Spirit, made known the coming salvation and the details surrounding it looked into it very carefully and diligently for themselves. When would it happen and what would the circumstances be?

One might imagine that they were hopeful this salvation would be for their time. This could be the very reason it was necessary for God to reveal to them that what they spoke was for a later time than their own. It was for our time. Yet, we can rejoice that this salvation extends to all that have believed, regardless of when they lived. The message of this salvation is associated with the sufferings of Christ prophesied by the prophets. This is exemplified in the suffering servant passage of Isaiah 53, which Peter later expounded upon. They also spoke of the glories that would come after Christ's sufferings. This includes his resurrection and heavenly glorification. After all their searching and inquiry, it was revealed to them that they were serving us with their words, this good news announced by the Holy Spirit whom God sent from heaven to inspire these prophets.

Furthermore, we see that the angels of heaven desire to look into these things. The image Peter paints for us is one of angels stooping down to see something of great importance, peering into the world of humanity just like we might look with wonder into a storefront window, full of Christmas celebrations and decorations, with gifts gleaming in colorful lights. They are stooping down and looking with intent observation at the details of our salvation. In it, they see the glorious working of God's hand. One must not presume that the angels have envy toward our special salvation, but rather they are full of wonder at the glorious work of God whom they praise.

Practical Response to Our Glorious Salvation

> Therefore girding up the loins of your mind, being fully sober, set your hope on the grace that is to be brought to you at the revelation of Jesus Christ.
> —1 Peter 1:13

This salvation, which both prophets and angels have desired to understand, gives us a hope for the future. All that Peter has presented in the preceding verses is now brought to conclusion by the word *therefore*. Since we have this salvation, we are to prepare for action. Peter gives us a word picture of one girding up a robe and tying it off around the waist so it does not get in the way while working. In this manner, we are to prepare our minds, literally each one of us tying up the loose ends of our mind and thoughts.

There seems to be a progression of action here that culminates in the exhortation to hope. The phrase "girding up the loins of your mind" might be better understood (using the Greek text as a guide) as something that precedes and prepares one for a life of hope, while "being completely sober" is concurrent with the act of our hoping in God's grace. Gathering up the loose ends of our minds leads us to mental sobriety. Keeping this image in mind, we can better see the progression when we read: "Therefore, after having girded up the loins of your mind, and being in a state of complete sobriety, hope in the grace to be brought to you in the revelation of Jesus Christ." Two more times, chapters four and five, Peter directs his readers to mental sobriety, a concept of great importance for him, that affects our walk with God and others.

Soberness is a state of mental alertness and purposeful focus that implies much more than sobriety from alcoholic drunkenness or chemical drug abuse. Loss of sobriety may occur through distracting obsessions or pleasurable preoccupations—anything leaving one in a mental fog or fantasy. It is in this state of preparedness and soberness that we are to hope. Specifically, we are to hope for the grace that is brought to us when Jesus is revealed. Our hope is real and not fantasy. The very condition of the imperative to hope is founded upon being sober-minded, mentally prepared, and alert. What areas of your thought life challenge your mental sobriety? Make these the subject of prayer, surrendering them to the grace of God.

The Call to Holy Living

> As obedient children, you should not be conformed to the former lusts when you were without understanding. But as he who called you is holy, you also be holy in every act of living. For it has been written "You shall be holy because I am holy."
>
> —1 Peter 1:14–16

We have been brought into a great salvation and are called to live in such a way that fosters fellowship with God and reflects his character. He is holy and desires us, his children, to be holy. We are called to live as obedient children of God. We were once, by nature, characterized by disobedience outside the covenant of God. Yet, obedience now is our character, and we are called to resist being conformed to the desires of the past when we did not know God. Of course, we are still tempted and subject to disobey; otherwise, there would be no need for the exhortation not to be conformed to past desires. However, we have been changed; we have become the children of God. The apostle Paul said the same thing when he taught the church in Rome not to be conformed to the world.

> I beseech you therefore, brethren, by the mercies of God, that you present your bodies a living sacrifice, holy, acceptable to God, which is your

> reasonable service. And do not be conformed to this world, but be transformed by the renewing of your mind, that you may prove what is that good and acceptable and perfect will of God. (Romans 12:1–2, NKJV)

Both Peter and Paul exhort us to resist the desires that once dominated our lives, to resist their conforming forces, to be different, and, more than that, to be transformed. Peter exhorts us to holy obedient living. Paul says we are to be transformed by the renewing of our minds so that we can then understand and know the will of God. Let us be mindful of what we were and, how we are now different and, called to be even more different. Our former lives were characterized by desires without the knowledge of God and without sobriety of thought. But now, we can no longer live with such lack of understanding, since he has made himself known.

The controlling idea in this passage is the call to be holy, for God is holy—a holiness that is to pervade our lives and all our conduct. This, in fact, seems overwhelming, especially when our unholiness is so apparent. There is great room for progress in our moral life. Peter appealed to the Old Testament to complete his argument. Leviticus 11:44 and 19:2 declares that we shall be holy because he is holy, 19:2 being a direct quote from the Greek version of the Old Testament his readers used.[2]

---

2. (The language we find in the LXX-the Septuagint, a Greek translation of the Old Testament used by Peter's readers- and the Greek New Testament, concerning holiness is one of declaration, using a future tense, "you shall be holy." The

> For I am the LORD your God. You shall therefore consecrate yourselves, and you shall be holy; for I am holy. Neither shall you defile yourselves with any creeping thing that creeps on the earth. (Leviticus 11:44, NKJV)
>
> Speak to all the congregation of the children of Israel, and say to them: You shall be holy, for I the LORD your God am holy. (Leviticus 19:2, NKJV)

The word *consecration* does not clearly communicate the connection between the act of consecration and the result of holiness. Both consecration and holiness have the same Hebrew root word—*kadash*, which means to be holy. "To consecrate" conveys something that is done to one's self, and is a form of the verb "to be holy." In Leviticus 11:44, the people are exhorted to keep themselves from unclean animals so they would not be defiled. God blessed their outward act of obedience with the blessing of his own holiness. The people were already considered holy before the Lord. They were to maintain their holy position by abstaining from touching the unclean things. Similarly, we who have come to Christ and are born again

---

NT usage is a quotation from the LXX. The Hebrew uses the imperfect tense to refer to both a future reference and the imperative. Why does the LXX translate the Hebrew as a future tense rather than an imperative? Grammarians will say that the future can sometimes be used as an imperative. Expert Daniel Wallace suggests that this passage should be read as an imperative. This suggests personal responsibility in the pursuit of holy living.)

are also holy by virtue of the new birth and are also called to faithful obedience, holy living.

The question must be clearly asked. How do we become holy? Do we make ourselves holy, or is this the work of God in our lives? Yes, it is the work of God. Let's ask another question: Is there anything we can do to promote holiness in our lives? To this, we can also give a resounding yes, for Scripture answers this plainly for us: "Make every effort…to be holy," (Hebrews 12:14).

> Pursue peace with all people, and holiness, without which no one will see the Lord. (Hebrews 12:14, NKJV)

> Therefore, having these promises, beloved, let us cleanse ourselves from all filthiness of the flesh and spirit, perfecting holiness in the fear of God. (2 Corinthians 7:1, NKJV)

While we can pursue holiness, it is Christ himself who is our holiness. We have *responsibility* in the process but not the *ability* to make ourselves holy. Holiness is from God, but we are responsible to live out our God-given holiness in acts of obedience.

> It is because of him that you are in Christ Jesus, who has become for us wisdom from God—that is, our righteousness, holiness and redemption. (1 Corinthians 1:30, NIV)

Can we make ourselves holy? If holiness can be defined by obedience to a list of commands, then yes we can make ourselves holy by being obedient. But in the letters of Paul, we are made to understand that it was human inability to keep the commands that condemned humanity. Though we are called to obedience, following a list of prescribed behaviors does not change who we are; it merely changes what we do. I would submit that we cannot make ourselves holy, even by obedience to a list of commandments. However, unholy living, breaking the commands of God, makes us impure and in need of the cleansing love of God graciously made available through Christ. Again, we affirm that we have responsibility in the process of becoming holy (the process of sanctification) but utterly lack the ability to make ourselves holy. Our feet cannot stop a car speeding down the road, but without our foot on the brake, the car is not going to stop. We can consecrate ourselves to the Lord, making ourselves available to his sanctifying work, and he will make us holy. Holiness, like salvation, is the work of God in our lives, the sanctifying work of God, which is received by faith.

Living in Godly Reverence in View of God's Judgment and Redemption

> And if you call upon a Father who judges each person's work impartially, live the time of your life journey reverently, knowing that it is not with perishable things made of silver or gold that you were redeemed out of the vain way of life handed down to you from your ancestors. But you were redeemed with precious blood, as from a blameless and spotless lamb, Christ's own blood. He was foreknown before the creation of the world, and appeared in these last days for your sake. Through him you are believers in

God, who raised him from the dead, and gave him glory; so that your faith and hope might be in God.

—1 Peter 1:17–21

Life of Reverence

Peter shows us how we are to live; we keep in mind that God as our Father is an impartial judge. If you call upon a Father who impartially judges the work of each person, then live the time of your wandering in this life, in fear or reverence toward God. By this saying, he affirms God as one who will impartially judge without prejudice and, therefore, will not neglect the work you have done, whether good or evil. Therefore, we are to live a life that honors God while we live in this temporary world, passing through as being on a journey to another destination—our heavenly home.

Redeemed by Christ's Sacrifice

While we live in reverence to the Lord, remember that we were redeemed from the vain corruptible lifestyles we inherited, redeemed not with perishable things made of the best precious metals but redeemed with precious blood, like an unblemished and spotless lamb, the blood of Christ. Once again, imagery from the Hebrew Scriptures helps better understand Christ's sacrifice. Our sin was placed upon him; his blood purchased our redemption; his covenant was established by sacrifice.

There are many pictures of substitutionary sacrifices in the Old Testament that foreshadow the price paid for our sins. The animal sacrifices of bulls, goats, and lambs have been replaced. Those were offered regularly, but Christ was offered once for all time for all. Although his sacrifice will never be repeated, its effectiveness in our lives will never be depleted. What can wash away my sin? Nothing but the blood of Jesus.

Redemption Planned Before Creation

Peter continues his exposition on reverence for God by showing God's foreknowledge and plan for our salvation through Christ. He who was foreknown before the creation of the world was revealed in these last days for the sake of humanity. God was not taken by surprise by the sinful choices made by his creation. Satan, a rebellious cherub, and Adam, a willing participant in deliberate disobedience, brought spiritual decay and death. God planned a remedy before the act was committed.

Redemption would come through God himself. The eternal Son of God would become the son of man to redeem all of creation. His death would atone for our sin and rebellion. Through Christ, we have become believers in God who raised Jesus from the dead and gave glory to him. He gave this glory to Christ with a purpose—that our faith and hope should be in God. The exaltation of Christ through the glory of resurrection draws our attention to the awesome wonder of the Father to whom we ultimately direct our faith and hope. Remember, he is our Father, the Father whom we call upon. Will you call upon him now?

Obedient Purifying Love and New Birth through the Word of God

> Having purified your souls by obedience to the truth, so that you have an un-hypocritical brotherly love, love each other persistently, out of a pure heart. Do this because you have been born again, born not of perishable seed but of imperishable, through God's living and abiding word. For all flesh is as grass, and all its glory like a flower of the grass. The grass withers, and the flower falls, But the *rhema* word of the Lord abides forever. And this is the *rhema-* word which was preached to you.
>
> —1 Peter 1:22–23

Consecration to the Lord through Loving the Christian Family

In response to our redemption, we are exhorted to love fervently and persistently. Having purified our souls (consecration) through obedience to the truth, which results in brotherly love that is without hypocrisy, we are to love one another earnestly, fervently, and persistently out of a clean heart. Our hearts have been purified by the blood that Jesus shed; we have been purified through faith because of his sacrifice. Obedience to the truth that purifies us is our faith in what God has done in and through his Son, whom he appointed and sent. Our love is purposeful, deliberate, and in direct response to his love for us. Obeying God's directive to love the brotherhood of believers brings a consecration to our lives that reflects his glory to the world.

Verse 23 gives us further reason for the directive to brotherly love. *You have been born again!* We are born anew not out of perishable seed but of imperishable through the living and abiding Word of God. The Scriptures portray God as one who creates with his powerful Word. He speaks, and it is so. It is no different with us as a new creation. His Word has been planted within us, and it has brought forth life. How can we not love our brothers and sisters who are also born of the eternal Father? For certain, love can be challenging, but God has enabled us with love beyond our own. We need only to obey the command to love, and he will empower us beyond our own ability, beyond our imaginations. His Word is imperishable and produces an imperishable life within us, an enduring Word that communicates his very life.

What does Peter mean when he said that we have purified our souls by obeying the truth? One can understand that obedience to God's truth would lead to love of the brotherhood (Christian family). Love is the fulfillment of God's law, but very simply, it is the obedience of having faith in Jesus Christ that has resulted in the purification of our souls. This faith subsequently results in the outward manifestation of love for the brethren. The apostle John indicates that if we have the hope of Christ's return in our hearts, we purify, sanctify, and set ourselves apart as holy, just as Christ is holy: "All who have this hope in him purifies himself, just as he is pure" (1 John 3:3, NIV).

While holiness and sanctification in terms of godly character are from God and the work of God, we can and are called to consecrate ourselves, making choices that are characterized as obeying the Word and direction of God. We do not make ourselves holy by obeying God, but we do offer ourselves up to God with our obedience, surrendering our lives as offerings to God and sanctifying ourselves to him so that he may sanctify us for himself. One might say we choose to be holy by what we do and how we live our lives in obedience; however, it is God who makes us holy by his work so that our souls may be pure, sanctifying us and making us holy on the inside.

We must also recognize in this passage that Peter is not telling his readers to purify their souls, but that they have already done so ("…now that you have purified yourselves…"). The result is sincere brotherly love, and, therefore, he calls them to actively and fervently love one another. Peter further regards this new propensity to love and the call to love as resulting from the new birth. We are part of God's family with new family benefits and responsibilities.

There seems to be a connection between obedience to the truth and being born again in this passage. In fact, obedience to the truth here is obeying the call to believe in Christ. It is through this saving faith that one has "purified himself," not obeying the commands of dos and don'ts. It is the response of faith to the Gospel of Christ out of a clean heart so that we may fervently love one another. Who is on your target list of love?

The Word of God Brings New Birth

As the apostle John said, we have been born again not of man but of God (John 1:12–13). Here in verses 24 and 25, Peter says the same thing in a different way. All flesh (humanity) perishes like grass, and the glory of humanity is even briefer, like when a flower falls, but the word (*rhema*)—the very *rhema* that was preached to them—of God abides forever. Peter quotes this from Isaiah 40:8 (LXX).[3] The Hebrew Scriptures, while communicating the same basic idea as found in the Septuagint, gives a slightly more colorful word picture for us, translated from the Hebrew: "The grass has withered, and the flower has drooped over, but the word of our God stands forever." Observe the contrast between the drooping flower and the forever upright Word of God.

When Peter says that all flesh is like grass, he is speaking of all humanity having a brief existence, all the glory of humanity is like a flower of the field, which is even shorter. Grass dries up, and the flower falls to the ground. Every year, I see the grass in my yard turn brown and die. The flowers in the grass and of most plants and trees are beautiful in the spring but are so brief. Human life lasts longer than seasonal grass, but our bodies are mortal; they will die. However, God has a greater life

---

3   The Septuagint translation of Isaiah 40:8 and the Greek version of 1 Peter 1:25 read very similarly with one word change "the word of our God abides forever" to "the word of the Lord abides forever."

for us. We have been born of his imperishable seed. That which is born of this world is temporary and perishing. That which is born of God is eternal. His eternal Word has been seeded into our hearts and yields eternal life. This is the eternal and imperishable Word delivered to us.

Chapter 2

Put Away Vices and Crave the Spiritual Nourishment of the Lord

> Therefore after putting away all malice, all deceit, hypocrisies, envyings, and all slanderings, like newborn babies, long for the pure spiritual milk, that by it you may grow in salvation; since you have tasted that the Lord is good.
>
> —1 Peter 2:1–3

Vicious Vices

Peter expands our vision on how we are to live out our relationship with God. In response to this living Word and the new birth, we are to shed the old ways of evil and badness, deceit, hypocrisies, jealousies, and every kind of slander. Some of these vices are referred to using plural words, emphasizing the many forms these old ways of life manifest themselves. Each of these vices has many manifestations. Even malice and deceit will manifest themselves in more than one way. Shall a Christian have a disposition of wishing evil to happen to another? No! Even Jesus said that we should bless those that curse us. Shall we be liars and deceivers? Yet, how many of us have lied about something or other since we were saved? Interesting that Peter had not said they already have put these vices away, but rather they are exhorted to do so. Avoid hypocrisy, not pretending to be someone other than who you are. There is no life or fellowship with God in such behavior. It is better to be rejected by others for who you really are than to be accepted for someone you are not.

While people may reject us, God has given assurance that he will never leave us nor forsake us. God knows our hearts. Surely, we know this and that he has accepted us. Others, however, often do not know us well enough to see our hypocrisy, while others do. Yet, we avoid hypocrisy not because we are watched by men but because we are seen by God. We are seeking to glorify God, not win the approval of people. Shall we live lives of envy when the God of the universe is our provider and every good gift comes from him? I have found myself fighting envious feelings, as perhaps you have as well. We envy over jobs, money, power, prestige, relationships, position, and popularity, and even over ministry! Put envy to death by turning to your covenant God who has revealed himself as *Jehovah Jireh*, the God who sees and so provides.

Slander is often connected with envy. Many slander because they wish what another has and so speak with evil intent. These vices often manifest as lifestyle behaviors that root themselves in life patterns. Each vice is foreign to the character that God works in us. However, they can be identified, confessed, and repented of. Diligence must be applied to putting off these vices, for they are enemies to spiritual growth. Let us learn contentment and gratitude for everything that God has provided. If you lack anything, ask God. In this way, you can battle envy that leads you to slander.

Crave Pure Spiritual Milk and Grow

In contrast to the old way of life, we are like newborn babies, those born of the Word of God and who are now the children of God. We are to desire and long for the pure spiritual milk that will make us grow. Some translations describe this pure milk as being itself the Word of God. The Greek word *logikon* (translated as *spiritual* or *word*) does indicate that this milk is not physical milk, but this of course can be ascertained from the context of the passage. *Logikon* is used only one other time in the New Testament, in Romans 12:1, where Paul used it concerning our reasonable or spiritual worship. J. Ramsey Michaels suggests it is not likely to mean spiritual in 1 Peter but rather simply describes this pure milk as symbolic.[4] This, however, does not diminish the value and greatness of this nourishment that God gives us. This

---

4. J. Ramsey Michaels, 86-88.

milk is not identified specifically, but it is clear that we are to desire as life-sustaining the pure things of God. This could certainly include the Word of God for our consumption but not to the exclusion of the many other pure gifts that come from God that sustain us. Edmund Clowney suggests in his commentary that reference to Scripture as the pure milk is what is intended.[5]

With the exhortation to desire this pure nourishing milk, we are given both the reason for this desire and the result of our consuming it. The result is growth and increase in our salvation. Throughout the New Testament and 1 Peter, our salvation is portrayed as both now and future. We are saved now, and yet the complete manifestation of salvation is still unfolding. In agreement with Peter, Paul shows the contrast between our reconciliation to God that is complete with the future orientation of our salvation. Romans 5:10 (NKJV) says, "For if when we were enemies we were reconciled to God through the death of His Son, much more, having been reconciled, we shall be saved by His life."

We have been reconciled (past), and we shall be saved (future). We are God's children, born again and reconciled to him. That is a done deal. However, the fruitfulness of our salvation is increasing. In fact, the word *grow* is often translated as "increase" and "be fruitful." I think we often confuse the idea of reconciliation and salvation. We often speak of our reconciliation as our salvation, while Scripture separates these terms. Our salvation is sure and secure in Christ. However, we know that our

---

[5] Edmund Clowney, 78-79.

resurrection will be the final phase of our Salvation; salvation is ongoing.

Peter concludes this part of his exhortation with another "if" statement. He exhorts us to desire this pure nourishing milk from God so that we may increase in our salvation, *if* we have tasted that the Lord is good. The expected answer is "Yes, we have tasted that the Lord is good." Peter has no doubt that those who have tasted the Lord's goodness will agree with him. Only the one who has not been redeemed has yet to taste the goodness of God. We have experienced the goodness of the Lord and will keep obtaining our nourishment from him. This will ensure the continued growth and fruitfulness of our salvation. May we continue to hunger and thirst after righteousness so that we may be filled. Christ is our righteousness.

Christ Is the Living Stone upon which the Church Is Founded

> You come to him who is a living stone. He was rejected by men, but with respect to God, he is chosen and precious. And you yourselves, as living stones, are being built to be a spiritual house, to be a holy priesthood for the purpose of offering spiritual sacrifices, acceptable to God through Jesus Christ.
>
> —1 Peter 2:4–5

After having been born again and now growing up into our salvation, Peter takes us further into our priestly worship of God that is founded upon the Lord Jesus himself. We have been exhorted to put off the vices of the old life and to desire what is pure to nourish us. Now Peter lays the conceptual foundation for our priestly worship. After exhorting us to appropriate living in the previous passage, here he gives detailed conceptual description of our priesthood.

We have come to Christ our Lord who is a living stone, and we keep coming to him in fellowship and faith. He was rejected but is the very stone that God chose and considered precious. The Father is the master builder; mankind is without proper knowledge of the things of God. Jesus is the foundation for the Church. He is the very rock that the Father has laid. The leaders of Israel rejected him as Messiah, cast him aside, and crucified him. They chose to build their own kingdom with their own foundation, tossing aside the only rock that would secure them. All who reject Christ today have committed the same damnable blunder, but there is still hope for those who reconsider.

Jesus, the very foundation stone, the living stone, has also made us to be living stones. We are being built and assembled into a spiritual house. It can never be overstated, it is not the building that is the temple; the people are God's temple. The people of the church are the stones that have been constructed to be a spiritual place of worship. Peter identifies us with our Lord Jesus Christ. He was a living stone, and so are we—living stones in a collective relationship with one another for the worship of the living God.

We have been assembled to be a holy priesthood with the very purpose to offer spiritual sacrifices of worship and service. These sacrifices are acceptable to God through Jesus Christ alone. He is the living stone, but he is also the high priest of our faith. He is the chief priest, and we serve as his priests. He is the one who approves our sacrifices. Our service is performed within the bounds of his will and orchestration.

Three months after God led Israel out of the land of Egypt, he spoke to them through Moses and gave them a promise. This promise was that if they would keep his covenant, they would be his treasured possession and be a kingdom of priests and a holy nation. It was God's desire that they all be like priests worshiping and serving him so that each would have the most intimate relationship as much as possible with Him.

> Now if you obey me fully and keep my covenant, then out of all nations you will be my treasured possession. Although the whole earth is mine, you will be for me a kingdom of priests and a holy nation. (Exodus 19:5–6, NIV)

The concept put forth during the reformation, the priesthood of all believers, is not new; it is the very Word of God. It is only now in the Church that this promise can be fulfilled. We are not a Church with one priest, rather we are an assembly and congregation of priests, built and chosen for holy worship. The apostle John declared that Christ has made us to be a kingdom and has made us priests to God. Moses spoke of this in terms of the future. John the apostle spoke of it as something completed in the past: "…to him who loves us and has freed us from our sins by his blood, and has made us to be a kingdom and priests to serve his God and Father—to him be glory and power forever and ever! Amen." (Revelation 1:5–6, NIV). And again, John asserts this truth.

> And they sang a new song saying: "You are worthy to take the scroll and to open its seals, because you were slain, and with your blood you purchased for God persons from every tribe and language and people and nation. You have made them to be a kingdom and priests to serve our God, and they will reign on the earth." (Revelation 5:9–10, NIV)

Christ the Cornerstone in Whom We Trust

> It is contained in Scripture, "Behold, I lay in Zion a stone, a precious chosen cornerstone, and he who believes upon him shall NOT be ashamed."
>
> —1 Peter 2:6

Scripture is the foundation for Peter's teachings. He learned the truth from Christ, yet he still appeals to the Old Testament Scriptures time and again, from which he continues to proclaim Christ, even expounding on the Word concerning him, so that we may put our faith in Jesus. By believing in him, we will in no way be shamed or disappointed. Our relationship to Christ is one characterized by faith from beginning to end. In fact, through faith there is no end!

The Greek language underlying our English translations here uses a double negative to emphatically assert that we will not be ashamed; our hope will never fail us.

The translation of the text here uses a capitalized NOT as an attempt to indicate this emphasis. We might further say that the one who trusts in him will in no way be ashamed. If we lay our lives on the line, putting our faith in Christ, we will not be shamed as if we had put our hope on an empty promise. He is our rock and firm foundation that will support us throughout eternity.

Several passages from the Hebrew Bible discuss how God placed his chosen precious stone (his Son) as the cornerstone, the firm foundation for his people. These are the passages Peter has expounded upon. Both Isaiah 28:16 and Psalm 118:22 declare that God would lay a foundation stone, one rejected by men but chosen by God. Paul in Romans 9:33 and Ephesians 2:20 declares the same.

> So this is what the Sovereign LORD says: "See, I lay a stone in Zion, a tested stone, a precious cornerstone for a sure foundation; the one who relies on it will never be stricken with panic." (Isaiah 28:16, NIV)

> The stone which the builders rejected has become the chief cornerstone. (Psalm 118:22, NKJV)

> As it is written: "Behold, I lay in Zion a stumbling stone and rock of offense, and whoever believes on Him will not be put to shame." (Romans 9:33, NKJV)

> Having been built on the foundation of the apostles and prophets, Jesus Christ Himself being the chief cornerstone. (Ephesians 2:20, NKJV)

A brief note should be made concerning the difference between Isaiah 28:16 and 1 Peter 2:6, which is reflected in a comparison between the KJV and the NIV. As usual, Peter quotes from the Septuagint from which we read "He who believes upon Him shall not be shamed," while from the Hebrew we read "He shall not make haste." We should further note that both Peter and Paul quote from the Septuagint in referencing this passage. Too much should not be made of this difference, except to iterate that the recipients of this letter are readers of the Greek language and would read the Greek translation of the Hebrew Scriptures, which at times result in emphasizing different ideas conveyed by the passages. In his commentary on Isaiah, Delitzsch translates "shall not make haste" as "will not have to move." Here the idea conveyed from Isaiah in the Hebrew Scriptures is that when there is impending disaster, the one who has the Lord for his foundation will not have to make haste and leave; he will not be shamed by having to run away to safety. The Lord is his rock and fortress of protection. Remember the old hymn "On Christ the Solid Rock I Stand"?

Jesus—Precious to Believers but a Rocky Road for Unbelievers

> Therefore, this precious one is for you who believe, but to unbelievers, a stone which the builders rejected. He became the head cornerstone, a stumbling stone and a rock of offence. They stumble by disobeying the word, to which they were also appointed.
>
> —1 Peter 2:7–8

Jesus is our foundation both for the individual and the corporate life of the church and the apex of its construction. Foundations are laid so that a structure may be built upon it—in this case, the church. Here a contrast is made between those who believe and those who do not believe. Believers received Jesus as a precious cornerstone, the very foundation of life and its crowning apex of completion. Unbelievers, who have rejected Christ, rejected the only secure foundation for their lives. Christ is the most important stone within the building of anyone's life. Those who reject this stone, throwing it away, will trip over it and fall upon it. Jesus spoke of himself as a stone upon which people would fall, and one that would fall upon those who discard him (Matthew 21:41–44).

Those who reject him stumble by disobeying the Word. Disobedience is the stumbling; this is what they have chosen. What else is there left in life for those who reject Christ? Their only remaining purpose is for stumbling disobedience. This is the appointed purpose for those who reject their Christ. We must not conclude that God has appointed some for obedience and some for disobedience, not at all! Rather, it is that those who discard the Christ who shall themselves be discarded. God's grace has been extended to everyone so that they may rest upon the sure foundation of salvation—Christ himself. Rejection of this sure foundation is the act of disobedience that underlies all other acts of rebellion. However, should this one repent and accept this Living Stone, he shall be saved.

> He will be as a sanctuary, but a stone of stumbling and a rock of offense to both the houses of Israel, a trap and a snare to the inhabitants of Jerusalem. (Isaiah 8:14, NKJV)

> Jesus said to them, "Have you never read in the Scriptures, 'The stone the builders rejected has become the cornerstone; the Lord has done this, and it is marvelous in our eyes'"? (Matthew 21:42, NIV)

God's Chosen People

> But you are a chosen race, a royal priesthood, a holy nation, a people owned by God, so that you may proclaim the praises of the one who called you out of darkness into his marvelous light. Formerly you were not a people but now you are God's people. You were outside God's mercy but now you have been shown mercy.
>
> —1 Peter 2:9–10

The people of God are contrasted with those who have rejected Christ the Rock. We are not like those builders who mistakenly or foolishly discarded their only hope for a permanent foundation. We are now firm and secure in Christ. In Christ we have been made into a chosen race, a royal priesthood, a holy nation, a people of his possession, belonging to him. The purpose for God choosing us is that we may proclaim his praises and greatness. Praise him who called us out of darkness into his marvelous light. They who were once not a people (showing his main audience was not Jewish) are now God's people. We were not among those who had initially received God's mercy, but now we have been "mercified" by God. God has had mercy upon us.

While at one time the Hebrew people were the only chosen race, we who are the children of Abraham through faith are now the chosen race of God. We are his people; he is our king. We are a kingdom of priests. This is not a new idea, but rather a very old one. From the beginning, God desired all of his people to be his priests, both men and women, not just one tribe of Israel. "You will be for me a kingdom of priests and a holy nation. These are the words you are to speak to the Israelites" (Exodus 19:6, NIV).

However, the priesthood of all believers would not be fulfilled until the coming of Christ, when he establishes us as his people. We all are called to the priestly ministries of worship, praise, and intercessory prayer. We offer up the sacrifices of worship through faith in his name. We are his holy nation, a race of priests who are to show forth the holy nature of our God. He is holy, and we shall also be holy. We are a people belonging to him. He has made us to be his own inheritance, his prized possession, his family.

All God does he does with purpose so that we may know him and fellowship with him. Part of this fellowship is the declaration of his praises. We declare praises to God himself, and we declare them to this world, announcing his greatness and majesty, goodness and love. We declare the praises of this one who has called us out of darkness into his marvelous light. We were lost, but now we are found, blind but now we see, deaf but now we hear his voice calling and directing us. Light is now shining upon us, in us, and through us, his marvelous, awesome and glorious light. We are speaking of his inner light by which our souls are illuminated, the spiritual purity of his being that drives out the darkness.

Peter reminds his readers that they were at one time not a people, but that has changed. They were (and we also are) the people of God. Hosea, the prophet, declared that God would call those who were formerly not his people, his people.

> I will plant her for myself in the land; I will show my love to the one I called "Not my loved one." I will say to those called "Not my people," "You are my people"; and they will say, "You are my God." (Hosea 2:23, NIV)

It was his intention from the beginning that all should be his people. After the rebellion of mankind, he made provision for the repossession of his inheritance. His choosing of a people through his faithful servant Abraham was to bring light to the nations. Through Israel came the Messiah, who was the light, the very light to whom John the Baptist gave testimony, declaring him to be the Lamb of God that takes away our sins.

Peter now begins to more explicitly apply the principles he has laid down for his readers. Principles must lead to action to be relevant for life, ideas converted to implementation, concepts into action. These actions and behaviors are often presented to us as commands, imperatives, and directives. This is what we find in the next section of Peter's letter.

How to Live Out the Principles of God's Kingdom

Responsibilities in the Home and Church

> Beloved ones, I strongly encourage you, as strangers and travelers, to abstain from fleshly lusts, which war against the soul. I urge you that the way you live your of life, among the nations, should consist of goodness, so that when others slander you as evil doers, they might eventually glorify God as a result of the good works you do, when he makes his appearance.
>
> —1 Peter 2:11–12

Peter reminded his readers of the principle that they were strangers in the world, who were looking for a more glorious home. His first practical application of this principle has to do with the relationship of the Church to unbelievers, who were speaking against them. Peter has been laying down for us a theological foundation, principles of the kingdom, his ideological, conceptual worldview, a framework that will help us live lives pleasing to God. We are not what and who we used to be, rather we are now children of God and all that Peter has outlined for us. Keeping in mind this framework for life set before us, we are given specific ways to live out the will of God within the realm of our human relationships. We are given a new worldview, a new way to look at life and make decisions, to walk a life of obedience in the here and now.

With gentleness and without harshness, we are strongly urged to live lives having basic Christian goodness. First, he reminds us that we are aliens and travelers in this world. This is not our home, and we are passing through. We are not to be distracted by being engrossed in fleshly desires; we are to keep ourselves away from them.

While sin may be pleasurable for a season and the desires of the flesh enticing, we must remember that these desires are warring against our souls. The desires themselves become arrows of fire from the tempter. As war has been waged upon us, we must respond in kind, waging war in return. While Paul tells us to put on the armor of God, Peter has us to keep away from these fleshly lusts. Instead of engaging in corrupt behavior, let us conduct our lives defined as consisting of "good." The way we live our lives in the world among unbelievers is to have a reputable nature about it that is full of "goodness."

The words *good*, *bad*, *right*, and *wrong* are often used to describe behaviors, but they are ambiguous in description and often need more specific definition. While we may want Peter to elaborate in this passage what good conduct is to look like, we are seemingly left with something less defined. However, this is only for a moment, for Peter describes in great and specific detail what the nature of this good conduct is. We want and need "good" to be defined for us. This is exactly what Peter does as he specifically addresses personal behavior and lifestyle.

We are given a reason and motivation for this good behavior. It seems that the recipients of this letter were being slandered as evil doers by the unbelieving Gentiles they were living among. Good behavior was meant to correct the misunderstanding these unbelievers had about them, not merely to silence the slander. This good behavior was to result in a change within the lives of these unbelievers who were observing the Church and speaking against it. The goal of God was that through the good works of the Church these slandering unbelievers would speak different words; that, in fact, they would glorify God in the day of visitation, the day of Christ's return.

It is curious that the reference to giving glory to God in the future is the goal here as opposed to giving glory to God now. What we are to understand is that our lives, consisting of good works, will result in a change in the lives of slandering unbelievers. The goal is that they will give glory to God not only now or for a moment but for all eternity. Peter expresses himself at length to say that our lives may result in the salvation of these who are now opposed to God, and when he returns they may find themselves among the many people of God, giving glory to him. Perhaps, Peter was recalling the words of Jesus while he wrote:

> You are the light of the world. A city that is set on a hill cannot be hidden. Nor do they light a lamp and put it under a basket, but on a lampstand, and it gives light to all who are in the house. Let your light so shine before men, that they may see your good works and glorify your Father in heaven. (Matthew 5:14–16, NKJV)

Civil Responsibilities

> Submit to every human institution on account of the Lord, whether to the king as being supreme, or to governors, who have been sent by him to punish evil doers and to praise those who do good. For this is the will of God, that by doing good, you silence foolish human ignorance. Do these things as free men and do not use your freedom to do evil, but live as servants of God. Honor everyone. Specifically, be loving the brotherhood, fearing God, and honoring the king.
>
> —1 Peter 2:13–17

In the following passages, Peter gives even more detailed practical application by explaining with examples how we are to live out the theology and concepts he has placed before us. These are to be lived out through our relationships with one another in the church and within our communities. We are first exhorted to submit ourselves to every human created institution *ktisei*. This word occurs in nineteen other places in the New Testament translated as "creation." However, the popular versions (NIV, KJV, NKJV, NASB) give the following translations: NASB—every human institution, NIV—every authority instituted among men, KJV and NKJV—every ordinance of man.

J. Ramsey Michaels contends that *ktisei* should retain its definition as creation (meaning people) rather than institution as a form of government. His reasoning is that submission, as discussed in these verses, is to persons and not institutions. Remember, we are called to honor everyone, meaning persons. Furthermore, we see that submission to individuals is discussed throughout, not just a government institution. We are given a reason why we are to live in submission. It is because of the Lord. Our relationship with Christ demands our submission to one another and in the way he prescribes it.

Here the prescription appears to be submission to those in civil authority. Peter expands on this "human creation" or institution as being the king who has supremacy or his governing associates. Human governments are the creation of the people and are expressed in various forms. Nevertheless, these governments employ the labors of men and women. To these servants of that government, we are to show honor, respect, and submission.

First mentioned is the king, who is as one having the superiority. During the Roman occupation of the known world during Peter's writing, there were no kings in the land, except for rare situations such as Judea, where a king appointed by Rome was allowed. These, in the regions to whom Peter wrote, had no king other than Caesar, the civil leader of the governed world. Furthermore, submission was extended to his governors who are described as being sent by the king for the purpose of punishing evil doers and giving praise to those who do good. Pontius Pilate is an example of such governors. He was Caesar's representative in Judea. The point being made is easy to apply to our day; we have Christian duty to submit to and respect civil authority: the President, Congress, and the Judicial Branch. We should also include more local authorities: state and city authorities. We may or may not like how they do their jobs, but we can respect and honor what they stand for as a reflection of the authority of God in this world.

Outbreaks of persecution coming down from Caesar, particularly Nero, had not yet occurred at the time of Peter's letter. One might wonder if the king would have been mentioned if he were actively persecuting Christians at the time of this writing. Nevertheless, all authorities were to be honored, even if they treated the Church badly. The laws of the land typically are intended for the good of society, though admittedly failures do occur. However, Scripture considers civil authority as being appointed by God. Consider what the apostle Paul had to say: "Let every soul be subject to the governing authorities. For there is no authority except from God, and the authorities that exist are appointed by God," (Romans 13:1, NKJV). Governors were appointed to carry out the rule of law and represented the king (Caesar) to the people. Both punishment and praise would be handed out to those who earned it. Paul acknowledged the authority of the state to punish those who did wrong, even if it meant his own death!

> If, however, I am guilty of doing anything deserving death, I do not refuse to die. But if the charges brought against me by these Jews are not true, no one has the right to hand me over to them. I appeal to Caesar! (Acts 25:11, NIV)

However, we must acknowledge that not all laws favor the Church or individual Christians. In the case where civil law contradicts the revealed will of God, we must obey God, and yet do so in a way that is still respectful of established authority. When the apostles were ordered not to preach Christ, they respectfully declined and said, "We must obey God rather than man" (Acts 4:19, 5:29, NIV). We must be absolutely certain that there is a true contradiction to the will of God and be willing to accept the consequences for civil disobedience. I have recently heard (at the time of this writing) of a North Korean Christian passing out Bibles who was shot dead for doing so. Surely, he knew the potential consequences and regarded the preaching of the Gospel as dearer than his earthly life. However our governments are run, we must pray for them that the kingdom of God may continue to grow and expand, that souls be saved and God be glorified. Pray for those persecuted and condemned by the civil authorities who suffer around the world for such civil disobedience that they may obey the Gospel command of Christ.

The will of God is further described for us in verse 15, one of the many aspects of his glorious will, that by doing good we may silence the ignorant assertions of foolish people. The world will slander, accuse, and mock, but as we do the will of God, their foolish talk will be stopped. They are ignorant because they do not know God, and neither do they understand the Church. They are without spiritual knowledge and, therefore, act foolishly.

Peter elaborates on our good behavior with respect to our freedom in Christ, tying it in with our witness to the world. We are free in Christ, no longer bound under the penalties of the Law. However, in our living free, we should not and must not think that we have the liberty to do evil. Rather, we may freely live as servants of God. It is a mistake to think that God's grace extends to us the freedom to sin; rather, through grace we receive forgiveness when we do sin. It is through the grace of God that we are instructed for righteousness. Paul exhorts us that the grace of God teaches us to say no to ungodliness and worldly passions (Titus 2:11–12).

Furthermore, let our behavior include honoring everyone. We are to be respectful to all with whom we have relationships, whether saved or unsaved. Even to those who ask us to give a reason for the hope we have in Christ, we are to show respect as we answer their questions. Peter guides us from the general exhortation to honor everyone, to how we precisely live it out. With regard to our relationships within the body of Christ, those Peter refers to as the brotherhood of believers, we are to love them.

Our relationship with God is one of reverent fear. The depths of what the fear of God is should be saved for another book so we may give it due justice. However, suffice it to say that the fear of God, which Christians have toward their heavenly Father, is one best described as holy reverence characterized by love and obedience. And finally, we are again exhorted to honor the highest office of civil authority.

In summary, Peter lists a few short imperatives: submit yourselves to every human creation (institution) or authority. Honor everyone. The specific ways mentioned to honor others are subdivided as: love the brotherhood, fear God, and honor the king. I recall reading a story about a Christian garbage collector. During his early morning prayers, while driving his truck, he asked God to show him his authority. As he was impatiently waiting for a red light to change, the man decided to run the light since he saw no one around. Immediately, he was greeted with the flashing red lights of a police car. After receiving a ticket and the police gone, he sensed God speaking to him that he had just seen the authority of God at work in his life. Can you pray today that God would expand your perception of his authority in your life and how to better live out your faith?

Submission of Slaves to Masters: How Is This Relevant for Today?

> The domestic servants should be submissive to their masters with all reverence, not only to the good and kind but also to the crooked. For this is grace, if because of conscience toward God, someone endures pain of unjust suffering. For what kind of praise is it, if while sinning (against your earthly master) you are beaten and endure it? But, if you endure suffering for doing good, this is grace with God.
>
> —1 Peter 2:18–20

In these passages, Peter explained how members of the family unit are to relate to one another. He first addressed the household slaves. Although slavery is no longer part of the world culture, except in rare cases, much can be learned and applied by studying these several verses, which speak to the household slaves about obedience to their masters. After speaking specifically to servants, he makes a more general application of suffering to the

Christian life, focusing on the example given to us in the sufferings of Christ himself.

Worldwide, slavery is viewed as a human rights violation; however, there are forms of it that are extant today. Currently, the world condemns slavery, as we all should. While slavery does exist in limited fashion, it is predominantly an illegal trade. At the time Peter's epistle was written, half of the inhabitants of Rome itself were slaves, and slavery was prolific throughout the empire. These house servants were not employees; they were outright slaves who were bought and sold. We can better understand this passage if we avoid the temptation to apply this as an employee–employer relationship.

Application of this passage would be difficult, if not impossible, for anti-slavery cultures, except that Peter turns this specific situation into a general principle for Christian living. Let us first understand what Peter intended when he wrote this and then try to glean something for our own lives. These house servants, as they are called, were to submit to their masters and do what they were told. Their attitude was to be one of reverent fear and respect. Being afraid is not here in the mind of Peter, since there would be no fear in serving a good master. But whether the master was good and kind or crooked and mean, they still were to show respect and obedience. Their submission, reverence, and respect extended to evil and crooked masters as well as good ones.

Peter makes an astounding comment: "For this is grace." He is not referring to God's grace here, but rather graceful living. If someone endures the pain of unjust suffering because of his conscious relationship with God, he is blessed and praised by God. This is the kind of graceful living to which God calls us. It is also the very kind of circumstance that the flesh rebels against. Our worldly conditioned mind screams injustice. What kind of praise should a rebellious disobedient slave expect to receive if he is beaten for his sin against an earthly master? The answer is *none*. Again, this is an unthinkable situation for most of us to relate with. Such a beating would again be a violation of human rights and is offensive, yet in much of human history, such atrocities have occurred. Even more offensive is the beating of a slave who has done only good. We are told that if one endures this kind of unjust suffering, he is living a gracious life before God, one that brings honor to the Lord. It was gracious Christian living if a servant endured the pain and grief of suffering unjustly. We will understand further from Peter that submission and enduring unjust suffering in the context of any relationship, is for the purpose of being a witness, pointing to Christ. This is the purpose for such grace-filled living.

To This You Were Called

> For to this you were called, for even Christ suffered-on your behalf, leaving behind an example for you, so that you may follow in his foot prints. He committed no sin, neither was deceit found in his mouth. When he was reviled he did not revile in return, when he suffered he did not attempt to threaten, but handed himself over to one who judges justly. He himself bore away our sins in his body on the tree, with the result that by our

> dying to sins, we may live for righteousness. By his wounding you were healed. For you were like sheep being led astray, but now you have returned to the shepherd and overseer of your souls.
>
> —1 Peter 2:21–25

Unthinkable to our minds and experience, Peter says, "To this you were called," called to suffer injustice gracefully! Why should such a thing be? What is the basis and authority for such a claim? It is the authority and example of Christ's own sufferings, for even Christ suffered on our behalf and not because of his offenses—he had none. He left us an example that we should follow in his tracks, literally his footprints! It is his example we follow; Christ himself is the pattern for our lives.

Peter turns this example to a more general exhortation relating to every Christian. Enduring unjust suffering is not just for the Christian slave; Christ suffered and left an example for all of us. He committed no sin, and there was no deceit found in his mouth as he graciously endured unjustly. He was sinless and without fault, without offense. His purity is in sharp contrast with his suffering. We might cheer when the wicked are arrested and jailed, but not the righteous! We are filled with sorrow when the wicked impose themselves on the good. Jesus did not commit any sins. Not even by what he said did he incur guilt. He spoke only what the Father told him to speak. In his suffering, he did not corrupt himself by cursing his persecutors; rather, he prayed for them. The prophetic word of Isaiah predicts this graciousness of Christ. "He was assigned a grave with the wicked, and with the rich in his death, though he had done no violence, nor was any deceit in his mouth" (Isaiah 53:9, NIV).

When he was reviled, he did not revile in return; during his suffering, he did not make any threats. Rather, he handed himself over to the righteous judge—his Father. The apostle James tells us that if someone does not offend by what he says, he is a perfect man, able to bridle his whole body (James 3:2). Christ's disciplined love gave him strength and motivation to refrain from speaking any deceitful words. His merciful love was extended to us from his cross. The way of the world is that one evil deed is returned with another evil deed, retaliation, eye for an eye, or worse. Though we live in a world that demands "tit for tat," Christ calls us to bless when we are cursed, to bless those who curse us, pray for those who use us despitefully. Like our Lord, we are in need of handing ourselves over to the righteous judge, our Father God. Surrender to him, entrust the life of our very souls to him during times of unjust suffering.

He bore away our sins. Peter elaborates beautifully about the meaning of Christ's sufferings on our behalf. He himself bore our sins in his body on the tree; bore them so as to take them away from us by transference. Our sins were placed upon him like the scapegoat sent away into the wilderness (Leviticus 16:10). Here we must pause and gaze upon the sufferings of our Lord with reverent awe and terror. Crucifixion itself was a terrible means of death, but Christ himself prophesied of his death in this way. He was not surprised. Yet, our sense of terror is not in the means of his death by crucifixion, but rather the realization that he has born our sins, those sins that would result in our eternal demise. Peter's words remind us of Paul's discourse about the cross of Christ. It was by this cross he took upon himself the curse, for cursed was everyone who hung on a tree (Galatians 3:13). This is why Peter takes us to the tree as the place where Christ bore our sins. The scapegoat is a figure of Christ bearing our sins, but on the cross, Christ literally bore our sins as he suffered under the curse, on our behalf.

The result of this act of mercy, love, and grace is that we who have died to sins through his death may live for righteousness, for by his wounding we were healed. Through his wounds, we may live a new life. While the popular translations, both for the Old and New Testaments, translate *wounds* in the plural, it is actually in the singular, meaning *wound*. This is not likely to be a collective singular (like fruit), since it does occur as a plural elsewhere. Christ's sufferings were many, but here we are to understand his complete suffering as a unified, whole experience.

The context of this passage must be understood to accurately understand Peter's quote of Isaiah. Here Peter references Isaiah 53, speaking to the sufferings of Christ and the effect they have upon our lives. Specifically, the healing of our souls is here referred to and can be verified from the context of Peter's message. Many claim this as a mandate for physical healing, while others insist this passage shows that Isaiah only meant spiritual healing. What is the answer? Peter's use here is spiritual healing, our salvation purchased through his suffering. However, Isaiah 53 speaks to both physical and spiritual healing. When Jesus was healing the people, as recorded in the New Testament, the apostle tells us these physical healings were a fulfillment of Isaiah 53 (Matthew 8:17).

We must remember that for the Israelite, healing and forgiveness both came from God, being bound together. Forgiveness resulted in healing. Salvation was understood to be a complete work rescuing both body and soul. When Jesus prophesied his death on the cross, he made reference to the Old Testament passage, where a bronze snake was lifted up upon a pole for the people to look at and trust God for their healing. They had been disobedient, and by this sign God gave them an opportunity to repent (spiritual healing) and be healed of the poisonous snakebites (physical healing). Extensive elaboration on this important topic cannot be done here, but I believe the point has been made. Isaiah 53 speaks to complete and whole salvation affecting body and soul, but Peter is here emphasizing the aspect of the soul's salvation. Joyfully, we can read and recite the forgiving and healing power of the sufferings of Christ, who provides salvation to us as the *shalom* of God, that peace which brings salvation as both spiritual and physical healing.

> He is despised and rejected by men, A Man of sorrows and acquainted with grief. And we hid, as it were, our faces from Him; He was despised, and we did not esteem Him. Surely He has borne our griefs And carried our sorrows; Yet we esteemed Him stricken, Smitten by God, and afflicted. But He was wounded for our transgressions, He was bruised for our iniquities; The chastisement for our peace was upon Him, And by His stripes we are healed. All we like sheep have gone astray;

We have turned, every one, to his own way; And the LORD has laid on Him the iniquity of us all. (Isaiah 53:3–6, NKJV)

The Torah (first five books of the Old Testament) uses the Hebrew word *chalanu* as a reference to sickness and is translated as "griefs" in Isaiah 53:4. Rarely is it used metaphorically, translated as "evil affliction," as in Ecclesiastes 6:2 (NKJV): "A man to whom God has given riches and wealth and honor, so that he lacks nothing for himself of all he desires; yet God does not give him power to eat of it, but a foreigner consumes it. This is vanity, and it is an evil affliction."

Isaiah's usage of the word in this Messianic passage refers to sickness and disease as demonstrated by Matthew.

> When evening had come, they brought to Him many who were demon-possessed. And He cast out the spirits with a word, and healed all who were sick, that it might be fulfilled which was spoken by Isaiah the prophet, saying: "He Himself took our infirmities And bore our sicknesses."(Matthew 8:16–17, NKJV)

Matthew makes clear that Isaiah 53 is not merely referring to spiritual healing. It was a fulfillment of the Messianic mission bringing wholeness to the entire person.

We were like sheep being led astray, led astray by the world, the flesh, and the devil. By the "world," I mean unregenerate humanity that would lead us down a path of destructive disobedience. The "flesh" is our own fallen passions and desires. The "devil" is that deceiver telling lies to distract us from believing and following God's truth. But now through Christ, we have returned, receiving him as the shepherd and overseer of our souls. We were lost, but now we are found, once without a shepherd, but now having the care of our loving Jesus who shepherds our souls and protects us from ravenous wolves that would devour us. No one can take us from his hand.

Chapter 3

The Relationship of Wives to Husbands and Their Witness

Likewise wives should be submissive to their own husbands, so that if anyone disobeys the word, they (the disobedient) may be won over, without a word, through the behavior of their wives, after they have observed your reverent blameless way of life. Let not your attraction be the outward braiding of hair and wearing of gold or putting on rich garments, but rather the hidden person of the heart, putting on the imperishable, a kind and quiet spirit which is of great value before God. For in this way the holy women of the past, who hoped in God, adorned themselves- by submitting to their own husbands. Sarah, for example, obeyed Abraham calling him lord. You have become her children by doing good and not fearing any intimidation.

—1 Peter 3:1–6

Peter now turns our attention to the relationship between the husband and wife, continuing the household code of conduct. First, he speaks to the wives beginning with "likewise." The question is: Likewise what? He just completed a lengthy discourse about household slaves, and one could misunderstand here a comparison between the wives and the slaves. This "likewise" refers to how we are to relate to one another with respect to God's will for our lives. He has great interest in how the Gospel is communicated through the witness of our daily social interactions.

The first reference to our social responsibilities having something to do with our relationship to God is found in chapter 2:13, "Submitting…on account of the Lord," and 2:19, "On account of consciousness of God," and verse 21, "Leaving an example behind for you." Peter continues the train of thought with "likewise" later referring in the chapter to how the husband is to relate to his wife. It is all for the glory of God and bringing testimony of him to the world. This is how we are to understand the directives guiding our family and social interactions.

This particular subject is difficult to address, since there is so much emotionally charged division over these issues of relationships between wives and husbands. The most pertinent question that comes to mind is how much of this concept—wives submitting to husbands—is purely cultural and how much is the sure Word and will of God? Can this be answered from the Scriptures themselves? We shall first examine the exhortations before us and then seek to establish their applications.

According to the Scriptures, wives are to submit themselves to their own husbands. Peter gives a most worthy reason for this. It is so that if any are disobedient to the Word they may be won over to Christ by the visible behavior of wives without a verbal word of the Gospel being spoken to them. Their reverent, blameless behavior can be seen and observed, itself pointing to God. A most difficult situation, both now and then, is the divided household where one is a believer and the other an unbeliever. This most often happens because one spouse is converted to the faith and the other is not. It was most difficult in the culture to which Peter wrote. It could be and often was an embarrassment to the husband who was still a worshiper of the gods of Rome. Further stress would occur when the wife would no longer participate in their routine sinful lifestyles. These issues still occur today. I have known devout women who, after coming to faith in Christ, no longer lived the sinful lives of their past. Their husbands subsequently abandoned them. The submission of wives to husbands is one of holy reverence to God, not to sinful compromise.

It has happened on many occasions that one's way of life solicited questions from unbelievers to find out what is different in their lives. How has Christ changed them? They want to know not out of simple curiosity but out of a hungry soul for fellowship with the living God, who seems real through the lives of his children. Behavior, within the context of a marriage relationship, can be a witness not only to one's spouse, but also to curious onlookers.

God looks at the heart of each person, while people look at the outside. They look to the strong and tall to be leaders. They look to young and beautiful women for satisfaction. What people are to see in the women of God are their beautiful hearts and spirits. While a woman may wear beautiful things, her beauty must be inward. God wants your beauty to come not from the way you wear your hair, the gold jewelry around your neck, your fine clothes, your expensive shoes, or exotic lingerie. These may all have their appropriate place, but it is not the clothes that make the woman but the spirit that is within her. It is the beauty of the hidden person of her heart, her gentle and quiet spirit that will not perish. Clothes and jewelry will perish. It is the redeemed spirit within that will endure. This is what God deems valuable. As seen by this passage, submission to the unbelieving husband is not based on the goodness of the man but rather the goal of winning him to Christ.

We must pause here and consider whether or not submission to a husband is merely an extension of a past culture, or if it is still within the framework of God's plan for the church today. Certainly, culture has changed much over these thousands of years. Today, slavery is anathematized. It would never be tolerated in our society and certainly not in the church. Yet, because of cultural considerations, it was tolerated in Peter's day. If wives are to have a submissive relationship today, why is slavery not permitted? What is the difference? First, the primary goal in this passage is so that an unbeliever may be won over. This can be an evangelistic relationship. God discourages believers from marrying unbelievers, but if they become saved while married they can win over their spouses.

Second, and perhaps more pertinent, is the example that Peter gives for submission. He appeals to the Old Testament women, specifically Sarah. These women of old adorned themselves by their submission to their own husbands. We know that Peter was not speaking with a Jewish community, yet he appeals to Jewish religious history to support the idea that wives should submit to their own husbands, an example from a different culture and a different time. Sarah is said to have obeyed Abraham and called him her lord. Those who follow her example are said to be her children; it is a characteristic of women in submission to God. In addition to this, such a woman will be doing good and not fearing any form of intimidation. Her good works come from her obedient submission to God. The nature of the marriage relationship changes when a husband or wife receives Christ as lord. The wife's most effective message is her behavior. Let us remember that the way she is to win the unbeliever over is through holy reverent kindness and quietness.

The exhortation not to fear any kind of intimidation is a curious addition to Peter's encouragement to wives. While this passage does not elaborate on the issue of fear, in the context of submission of wives to husbands, a few items come to mind. First, it could be a scary thing to show such submission to a husband, to the extent of calling him lord, as Sarah called Abraham and obeyed him, trusting someone else with your welfare. The other aspect, where fear may come into play, is the culture of the day. Within the Greek and Roman society, the god whom the husband worshiped was the god his whole household was to worship. A Christian wife might be a source of embarrassment for the husband if she were to serve a different god than he did. The wife could be intimidated by the consequences of her newfound faith in God, but she was encouraged not to fear the intimidation that might come her way.

Our witness must be culturally relevant and scripturally guided. Slavery was an integral part of Roman social structure and slaves needed to know how to live for Christ and be the best witness possible under those circumstances. Wives were in a socially subordinate position, both in Judea and in the Roman world. Wives also needed to know how to be the best witnesses possible under their repressed circumstance. Today, our culture is much different and not so oppressive, but there are still social expectations. Currently, optimal marriage relationships are viewed more as partnerships and cooperation rather than subordination. How can husbands and wives relate to each other, in contemporary culture, in ways that make their witness to Christ most optimal? We know that in Christ there is neither male nor female, slave nor free. We know that Christ has torn down the walls of racial barriers, placing everyone on an equal plane. Of course, we do not disband sexual identity; biology has clearly demarcated male and female. However, to the extent that Scripture encourages partnership in marriage, we should also emphasize this. This is how we can be both culturally relevant and scripturally grounded in our witness to the world, which is of utmost importance. The many people that surround us witness our lives. How we relate to one another is a witness to them. Jesus indicated that this was most certainly the case when he said, "By your love shall all men know you are my disciples." Whatever the cultural context, we live in love as a witness pointing to Christ. This is the guiding principle to all relationships, and especially marriage.

The Relationship of Husbands to Wives

> Husbands likewise, dwell together with your wife according to knowledge, with the wife as being the weaker vessel. Show her honor even as a joint heir of the grace of life, so that nothing may hinder your prayers.
>
> —1 Peter 3:7

Peter continues his earlier exhortation, which the whole household code is established upon: "Honor everyone" (2:17). Husbands are *likewise* to relate to their wives, keeping in mind their relationship with God and his will and living for his glory. Husbands are to live together with their wives according to *knowledge*. While Peter has a specific form of knowledge in mind, it is useful to consider a general application first. One of the many complaints married couples have is exactly this: "My husband or wife does not understand me," or "I just don't understand him or her." Both husband and wife would fare better in their relationships with each other by understanding one another better. After having taken personality tests with my spouse, I learned much more about her and was better able to understand her as well as myself. This actually helped build greater understanding and facilitate mutual acceptance. This will not solve all your problems, but it is a start! Use all the resources available to you, including your spouse. You might consider reading *The Five Love Languages* by Dr. Gary Chapman.

To what specific knowledge is Peter referring? The wife is described as the weaker vessel. This is what husbands are to keep in mind as they live in marriage with their wives. When we examine humankind, we see that in general men are stronger than women. Men have more muscle mass per body weight, more red blood cells per volume of blood, and they are on average taller. Is this what Peter is really addressing? Perhaps, it is part of it; the word *vessel* is often used to refer to the physical body. However, we can look around and see how men and women pair themselves up. Sometimes, the woman is bigger and stronger. For some couples, one would certainly not be able to say the wife is weaker physically, so how would this passage apply to them?

The goal of Peter's exhortation is that the husband is to treat his wife with special honor. Whether she looks weaker or not, treat her as a valuable vase that you do not want to break. Show honor to her as a fellow heir of the gracious gift of life; this is partnership. She is your fellow heir. Remember that in Christ there is neither male nor female. While the wife is exhorted to submit to her husband, the husband is to treat his wife as a mutual partner within the family structure. While it is true that we are in Christ now, we are also in a physical world and embedded in society's culture; our goal is to show forth

Christ within our culture. How we relate to one another is a witness to the world around us. Women's rights were not very good in ages past. Many would say we still have a long way to go. Nevertheless, she is a fellow heir on equal footing with respect to the eternal life God has for us. A husband has a special calling and anointing from God to minister life to his wife. He is to pray for her strength and for her purity. Marriage is a relationship where both partners can draw upon each other for strength and support in times of weakness.

A husband's very prayers are affected by how he treats his wife. Men can hinder their prayers by mistreating their wives. You cannot hope to help the world if you do not love your own wife. Living with your wife with this knowledge in mind and treating her with such honor will promote a more successful prayer life. Building the kingdom of God begins at home.

Directions for Everyone

> Finally, everyone be likeminded, sympathetic, brother loving, compassionate, humble, not repaying evil for evil or abuse for abuse, but on the contrary, with blessing. For to this you were called, so that you may inherit a blessing. For he who would love life and see good days, must restrain his tongue from evil and his lips must not speak deceit. He must turn from evil and do good. He must seek peace and pursue it. For the Lord's eyes are upon the righteous and his ears toward their prayer; but the face of the Lord is against evil doers.
>
> —1 Peter 3:8–12

Peter comes to the end of a section in his letter where he has just given very specific direction to groups within the church: slaves, wives, and husbands. Now he speaks more generally to everyone and marks the beginning of this discourse with "Finally, everyone." Peter immediately lists the behaviors and personal character to be within the people of God: like-minded, sympathetic, brother-loving, compassionate, humble, not repaying evil for evil or abuse for abuse but instead blessing. Each of these is worthy of special consideration.

As much as possible, we as a people of God are to have the same mind and think the same way. Yes, we are individuals with our own thoughts and uniqueness, yet what we are exhorted to here is unity of mind. Our unique gifts and thoughts are to be joined together to serve the whole of the body of Christ. Even in doctrine and faith, we are to have one set of beliefs, and this is the ideal. Of course, these are to be accurate beliefs of truth. The rest of Scripture exhorts us explicitly to this end. While we may concede that for all the people of God everywhere at all times this may never happen until we are in the eternal heavenly kingdom, we must also believe that we can do much better than we have. Greater unity awaits us, a unity for which we must labor and pursue. Other passages echo this unity of mind.

> All the believers were one in heart and mind. No one claimed that any of his possessions was their own, but they shared everything they had. (Acts 4:32, NIV)

> The mind governed by the flesh is death, but the mind governed by the Spirit is life and peace. (Romans 8:6, NIV)

> I appeal to you, brothers and sisters, in the name of our Lord Jesus Christ, that all of you agree with one another in what you say and that there may be no divisions among you, but that you may be perfectly united in mind and thought. (1 Corinthians 1:10, NIV)

> Finally, brothers and sisters, rejoice. Strive for full restoration, encourage one another, be of one mind, live in peace. And the God of love and peace will be with you. (2 Corinthians 13:11, NIV)

> In your relationships with one another, have the same mindset as Christ Jesus. (Philippians 2:5, NIV)

We are furthermore called to display sympathy toward each other, to love each other with brotherly love under the Fatherhood of God. We are to be a compassionate people showing extreme mercy. After compassion, we find the word *humble* (*tapeinophrones*), another rare word used only here in the New Testament and once in Proverbs and which literally means "humility of mind." Elsewhere in Scripture, we are exhorted not to be high-minded, not to think more highly of ourselves than we should, but rather to think soberly.

There are times we experience extreme challenges in life and in our relationships. We may be subject to evil and abuse. The world is often unkind, our companions sometimes hurtful. In response to evil and abuse, we are exhorted, "Do not return evil for evil or abuse for abuse." God makes clear to us his desires and will for our lives, and he gives us clear reasons why we should follow and pursue them. Here we are exhorted what not to do and then again what we are to do. We are not to repay evil to those who do evil to us. Neither are we to be abusive to those who would be abusive to us. On the contrary, we are to bless them. Remember the words of Jesus: Bless those who curse you and do good to those who despitefully use you. Why? Here is the good news: there is blessing when we bless! We bless those who do evil to us and abuse us because we were called to do so, just as Jesus did. It is the will of God that we bless everyone, even those who are against us. This presents an incredible witness of Christ to them, perhaps, even a sign that they may believe.

I remember driving to work in a rain downpour one morning. I had to merge into the right lane. I looked in my mirrors and out the back window, but it was raining so hard I could see nothing but rain. I had to depend on cars having their headlights on to see any cars behind me. I merged into the right lane, not seeing any headlights. Immediately, I heard the honk of a car directly behind me. He moved to the next lane beside me at the stoplight. I rolled down my window to tell him that if he had his lights on I would have been able to see him. He went off on me telling me, "Fine piece of driving!" and whatever else he may have said I don't remember. It did not take long for me to feel the anger well up inside of me, envisioning taking a turn right into his fine-looking car. Immediately, God brought to mind the words of Jesus, to bless those who curse you and pray for those who despitefully use you. Instead of returning abuse for abuse, in obedience to that Word, I began to pray for the blessing of God's salvation over his life.

A further purpose and result of our blessing others is that we may inherit a blessing. It occurs to me that the action of blessing others so that we may receive blessing may seem like we are earning the blessing. However, consider that we *inherit* God's blessing. Wages are earned, but an inheritance is received and not earned. First, the blessing we receive as an inheritance outclasses any blessing we give to others. Second, by blessing others we open the channel of God's blessings in our own lives. God is a God who blesses, and we show ourselves to be his children by doing what he does—blessing others.

We are given further direction how to live out our faith in very practical ways, continuing with verses 10–11: "For he who would love life and see good days, must restrain his tongue from evil and his lips must not speak deceit. He must turn from evil and do good. He must seek peace and pursue it." For the person who wants to love life and see good days, here are the keys.

He must stop or refrain from speaking evil, and his lips must not speak deceit or lies. Furthermore, he must turn from evil and do good. Works will follow the words we speak. Out of the abundance of the heart the mouth speaks, and this directs the kind of life we will each live. The words we speak must not be full of reckless babble that stabs at the heart or chronic complaints that corrupt the soul, but rather be wise and bring healing instead:

"The words of the reckless pierce like swords, but the tongue of the wise brings healing" (Proverbs 12:18, NIV).

"He must seek peace and pursue it," another practical exhortation. Offenses of speech are so common in our relationships, especially in our families. These promote separation and hiding from each other and are indicative of deeper issues of fear, mistrust, and, perhaps, other sins one is trying to hide. The remedy is to seek peace and pursue it. We have been given peace with God through reconciliation to him. We are to further seek peace with each other so that we may also be reconciled to one another. We seek it and look for it, and even more, actively pursue it. When we lose or misplace a large amount of money, we look for it, even mounting a vigorous search to find it. We don't stop until we have it in hand. In our search and pursuit for peace and reconciliation with each other, let us not give up till we have obtained it. It holds greater value than a wad of cash!

Some of Peter's directives carry with them the idea of a continued action. For example, doing good is not a one-time event but an ongoing lifestyle. Seeking peace is something we are to continue doing. Pursuing is not done once, but something very active and ongoing.[6] As

---

6. Each of these imperative commands is given in the Greek aorist tense. Remember that in the imperative mood, tense reflects kind of action rather than time of action (past, present, or future). The aorist kind of action generally gives a snapshot perspective, which means in this case that the actions of these commands are viewed as a whole, something that simply must be done. Peter's intent, at least from a grammatical point of

we have seen before, Peter often uses the Old Testament as the subject of his teaching, as he does here by referring to the following passages.

> Who is the man who desires life, And loves many days, that he may see good? (Psalm 34:12, NKJV)

> Turn from evil and do good; seek peace and pursue it. (Psalm 34:14, NIV)

None of our behaviors go unseen. Peter reminds us of this, recalling Psalm 34:15–16. The eyes of the LORD are upon the righteous, and his ears hear their petitions. However, God's presence is against those who do evil. We are given a choice on how we will live. What we do has consequences, and nothing goes unseen. Let us walk in faith and love, enjoying the covenant that God has made with us, seeking and pursing peace with one another.

> The eyes of the LORD are on the righteous, And His ears are open to their cry. The face of the LORD is against those who do evil, To cut off the remembrance of them from the earth. (Psalm 34:15–16, NKJV)

See these characteristics and exhortations as lifestyle changes to be integrated into your decision-making processes and worldview. God is transforming our lives.

---

view, is not to show an ongoing process per se but something that simply needs to be done. The verbs themselves however indicate a sense of continued action. The meanings of the words themselves indicate progressive action.

What If You Suffer for Doing Good?

> And who shall harm you if you become zealous for what is good? But even if, perchance, you suffer because of righteousness, you are blessed. Do not fear them and neither be troubled (or intimidated), but sanctify the Lord Christ in your hearts, always ready to give a defense to everyone who asks a reason for the hope that is in you. Reply with gentleness and respect, maintaining a good conscience, so that those who revile your good conduct in Christ may be ashamed of their slander against you. It is better to suffer while doing good than doing evil, if the will of God so desires.
>
> —1 Peter 3:13–17

Peter asks the question: Who shall harm you if you become zealots or champions of the good? Perhaps, we might prematurely answer, "No one." But Peter contrasts this idea with the truth that even if we were to suffer because of righteousness, we are blessed. *Suffer* is in the present tense, active voice but *optative mood*, and expresses the *remote possibility* that one would suffer for doing good. He is, in fact, speaking hypothetically. While for the most part one would not expect to suffer for doing good, it is possible, even if seemingly remote. It is helpful to remember that persecutions against Christians in the Roman world were isolated events at the time Peter wrote this epistle. Nero had not yet begun his persecution of the Church. Full-blown and extensive persecution of the Church did not occur until Nero, and even more so after the year 100 A.D. Yet, when it comes to the good we would do with respect to our relationship to Christ, the world may very well persecute us. We must remember the words of Jesus:

> Blessed are those who are persecuted because of righteousness, for theirs is the kingdom of heaven.(Matthew 5:10, NIV)

> These things I have spoken to you, that in Me you may have peace. In the world you will have tribulation; but be of good cheer, I have overcome the world. (John 16:33, NKJV)

We will not always know when such suffering will occur, but we do know that we will have tribulation in this world, and so we must prepare for it. The good news is that Jesus has overcome this world and now passes his victory on to us!

The last part of verse fourteen expounds Isaiah 8:12–13 and continues with the encouragement to be fearless in the face of godly suffering. Peter uses the LXX (Greek version of the Old Testament called the Septuagint) throughout his epistle and here lifts the passage almost verbatim.[7] We do not have to fear those who would seek

---

7. Compare the passage in Peter with Isaiah. 1 Peter 3:14-15, but the fear of them do not fear neither be troubled, but the Lord Christ sanctify in your hearts. Isaiah 8:12, but the fear of him do not fear neither be troubled, sanctify the Lord himself and Him shall you fear. These comparisons reflect the closeness between the Greek versions, and the dependence of Peter on the Isaiah text.

to cause our suffering. We must not fear them and not be troubled or disturbed by them. In place of fear toward any that would threaten us, we will rather sanctify Christ as Lord in our hearts, giving him the pre-eminence. Shunning the fear of man and trusting God is taking a stand to honor the Lord.

> Do not call conspiracy everything this people calls conspiracy; do not fear what they fear, and do not dread it. The Lord Almighty is the one you are to regard as holy, he is the one you are to fear, he is the one you are to dread. (Isaiah 8:12–13, NIV)

The Isaiah passage exhorts us that it is God whom we are to reverence. The Hebrew passage of Isaiah 8:12–13 reveals that the Lord being spoken of is YWHY (*Yaweh* or *Jehova*), and yet here Peter refers to Christ as being the Lord of this passage. Remember that Scripture tells us: "That all should honor the Son just as they honor the Father. He who does not honor the Son does not honor the Father who sent Him" (John 5:23, NKJV).

There is no conflict here by identifying Christ with *YWHY* or *Jehovah*, whom we are to honor, even as we honor the Father. Christ presents the Father to us not just in his message but in his very person. In place of fear, deep in our hearts we regard Christ as holy. God liberates us from the fear of man, for it is a snare to those who will follow the Lord (Proverbs 29:25). Instead, he gives us ever-increasing boldness that we may bear witness to his salvation.

Our faith will be challenged from time to time, facing intense opposition or, perhaps, just a simple inquiry. Either way, we are to be ready always to give a reply or defense to everyone who might question us about the hope that we have within us. Our reply to such questions is to be full of gentleness and respect, but never fear. By testifying of Christ to others in this way, we keep a good and clear conscience that will influence those who question us and who might even slander and revile us for our hope and way of life in Christ.

It is God's will that our lives bring the world to him. They will revile us, poke fun at us from time to time, and laugh, and even slander us. However, our behavior is to silence their taunting words and bring them to shame. If our lifestyles bring God glory through Christ, the world has a chance for repentance and salvation. May God help us that our lives do not hinder the advancement of the Gospel but clearly point the way instead.

Keep in mind that it is better to suffer for doing good rather than doing evil, if it is necessary, in order to contrast God's good to the world's evil. Immediately, the question comes to mind whether God would ever find such need. Certainly, our flesh would rise up and shout its resounding "No!" We must dispel that misconception. Peter takes us to the heart of the matter with the example of the sufferings of Christ that we are to follow.

John Robert Bracamontes

Christ's Sufferings:
Why Unjust Suffering Is to Be Endured

> For even Christ suffered, once for sins, the righteous one on behalf of the unrighteous many, so that he may lead you to God after being put to death in the flesh and made alive by the Spirit, by whom he also preached to the spirits in prison, who were formerly disobedient when the patience of God was waiting in the days of Noah, while the ark was being built. In it, only a few- eight souls, were saved, through water. This symbolic baptism now saves you also. It is not a removal of dirt from the body, but a request of a good conscience toward God. It saves you through the resurrection of Jesus Christ, who is at God's right hand. Who has gone into heaven, with angles and authorities and powers in submission to him.
>
> —1 Peter 3:18–22

Peter reminds us that even Christ suffered according to the will of God and on our behalf, once for all time concerning our sins. His sacrifice was complete, not lacking anything, a sacrifice that was once for all with no need of repetition. The only righteous one was given on behalf of all the unrighteous many with the purpose to lead us to God. His example of suffering encourages and strengthens us that we may endure for his glory. Peter embarks on a discourse concerning the sufferings of Christ that we may better understand them and be encouraged and rejoice in his completed work. After his work of suffering, followed by his resurrection effected by the Holy Spirit, he continues to lead us to the Father, bringing us into fellowship as children of God. Christ's sufferings have had a great impact within the human heart and mind, now as well as beyond the grave. His resurrection empowered his suffering to transcend this world into the next, to have redemptive power. Because of the resurrection, his suffering brings salvation.

The sufferings of Christ transcended this physical world, when he proclaimed the Gospel to those who died in the days of Noah. Although he was put to death in the body, he was made alive by the Spirit. It was by the Holy Spirit he was raised from the dead, and by that same Spirit he went and preached to those who were previously disobedient in the days of Noah, before the flood. God waited patiently during those days that he might bring salvation to Noah and his family.

Peter seems to make a diversion in his teaching, illustrating the flood as a symbol of purification. The ark is what saved them from the flood, but the water of the flood saved them from a corrupt world. They were saved through water,[8] indicating literally that they were saved through or by the instrument of the water. This passage tells us they were not saved from the water but through the working of the water itself, by what it did.

Verses twenty and twenty-one are often passed over and misunderstood. Our English usage of *through* can be confusing because we might understand it to mean that God saved them by taking them through the flood, as he would get us through a problem. We might also

---

8. *diesothesan di hudatos*–literally with the same word order as the Greek New Testament—"they were saved-through-water"

understand the word *through* in the sense that our salvation is through the blood of Jesus. It is the agency of the blood of Christ that works our salvation. Here we are to understand the word *through* to convey that the water was the way that God secured their salvation. What did he save them from? He saved them from the corrupt world that he was destroying. The water of the flood of Noah is a symbol of the water baptism that now saves us, not our redemption but our sanctification. Baptism is not redemptive but rather is a work moving us toward a sanctified life.

This is where many can get confused. When the word *salvation* is used, we usually think of being saved from our sins and saved from the punishment of hell. The blood of Christ accomplished that. Here Peter is talking about the working out of our salvation in terms of sanctification, becoming more like Christ. The flood was the symbol of the reality of our baptism. How does baptism save us? Through it, God continues his work of making us more like Christ.

Peter first tells us what baptism does not do and then what is does do. Our baptism saves us, not by the removal of dirt from the flesh or body; rather, he says it is the pledge and pursuit of a good conscience toward God. This bears repeating: Baptism is the pledge and pursuit of a good conscience toward God. What is the power behind baptism? Peter says it is the resurrection.

This act, empowered by the resurrection, is not just a symbolic dipping, nor does it cleanse us from our sins. The purpose of baptism is to pledge obedience to

God, putting to death the sinful flesh by faith in the work of Christ, and receiving this by faith through the resurrection illustrated by the act of baptism. Paul tells us we are buried with Christ in baptism and raised with him in newness of life. His resurrection life is what gives baptism its power. Christ's sufferings have brought great salvation to us and exalted glory to him through the resurrection. This is why unjust suffering can be patiently endured: it will bring a convicting witness to the world, eternal glorification to us, and exalted glory to God to whom we bear witness.

Peter takes us beyond the death and resurrection of Christ to his ascension into the heavens. We see him now at the right hand of God with all authority, having angels, authorities, and power in submission to him, whether they are earthly or heavenly powers, human or spiritual. Jesus said that all power and authority was given to him, and he subsequently passed that power and authority on to us. Passages from Daniel and the Gospels easily make the point.

> He was given authority, glory and sovereign power; all nations and peoples of every language worshiped him. His dominion is an everlasting dominion that will not pass away, and his kingdom is one that will never be destroyed. (Daniel 7:14, NIV)

> And Jesus came and spoke to them, saying, "All authority has been given to Me in heaven and on earth." (Matthew 28:18, NKJV)

> Then He called His twelve disciples together and gave them power and authority over all demons, and to cure diseases. (Luke 9:1, NKJV)
>
> I have given you authority to trample on snakes and scorpions and to overcome all the power of the enemy; nothing will harm you. (Luke 10:19, NIV)

Our authority, the right to command, does not come from human rights but rather from the hand of God. It is what is called "derived authority." This is a restoration of authority, given to humanity by God at creation to rule the earth as God's representatives, who bear his image. In Christ, the image of God is restored, and the authority to rule and administrate his will in the earth is renewed. Our salvation and sanctification have far-reaching effects.

Chapter 4

Victory Over the Sinful Nature

> Therefore since Christ suffered in the flesh, you also equip yourselves with the same mindset. For the one who suffered in the flesh has ceased from sin so that he no longer lives the remainder of his life in the flesh by human lusts, but by God's will.
>
> —1 Peter 4:1–2

Now that we have seen the sufferings of Christ, as they have been declared to us by Peter and by all Scripture, we can arm and equip ourselves with the same mindset as Christ. We will benefit from spending time meditating on the sufferings of Christ and being encouraged by his strength and commitment to the will of the Father, fathoming his love for us. His suffering becomes our suffering, and his strength becomes our strength. We are never alone in our sufferings because he is with us. When we suffer for his Gospel, we are blessed. When we suffer the trials of temptations, resisting the desires of the flesh, we are blessed, since by them we also participate in his sufferings as we resist. Having the mind of Christ and his perspective, we are equipped to endure and overcome.

The one who has suffered in the flesh has ceased from sin so that he no longer lives for human lusts but rather for the will of God throughout the rest of life. This concept, of having ceased from sin through suffering, has been discussed from several positions in the history of the Church. First considered is the personal suffering of each Christian in day-to-day life. Second is the identification with Christ's suffering and death through baptism. Identification with Christ through baptism seems to be the stronger possibility here because of Peter's previous discussion on baptism. Our identification with Christ's sufferings in baptism makes a stronger case than personal suffering does. Each of us has a different life path, some with more suffering than others. Yet, each of us can completely identify with the sufferings of Christ through faith as we submit to the cross, the burial of baptism, and being raised with Christ into newness of life. This is the imagery of baptism and the reality of our lives as we identify with Jesus. It is the work of Christ in us that will result in a sanctified life, not our personal individual sufferings. We are crucified with him, buried, and raised with him. The apostle Paul makes some remarkable statements that complement the words of Peter.

> What shall we say, then? Shall we go on sinning so that grace may increase? By no means! We are those who have died to sin; how can we live in it any longer?…anyone who has died has been set free from sin. (Romans 6:1–2, 7, NIV)

Though most translations repeat the wording "has been freed from sin," a more literal translation of the Greek New Testament would read "has been justified from sin." We still have the potential for sin, still can be tempted, but are no longer under its dominating power and no longer under its guilt and condemnation.

> Those who belong to Christ Jesus have crucified the flesh with its passions and desires. (Galatians 5:24, NIV)

> For you died, and your life is now hidden with Christ in God. ⁴ When Christ, who is your life, appears, then you also will appear with him in glory. ⁵ Put to death, therefore, whatever belongs to your earthly nature: sexual immorality, impurity, lust, evil desires and greed, which is idolatry. (Colossians 3:3–5, NIV)

Obedience to Christ: Our Way of Life

> You have spent enough time in the past living out the desires of godless nations, going about in debauchery, lusts, drunkenness, revelry, binge drinking, and forbidden idolatries. With respect to their desires the disobedient are amazed that you are not running around together with them into

> the same reckless excess. As a result, they revile you-making fun of you. They will give account to the one ready to judge the living and the dead. For this reason even the dead were evangelized- that they may be judged according to men in flesh but may live according to God by the Spirit.
>
> —1 Peter 4:3–6

It is enough, whether for a short or long time! It has been enough to spend any time in lustful desires, which those outside the faith pursue. Specifically named are: debauchery, lusts (sinful passions), drunkenness, revelry (idolatrous parties), binge drinking, and forbidden idolatries. For the most part, our experience in the United States does not include idolatrous worship of other gods (although there is some nature worship and Satanism). However, we are predominately guilty of self-worship and idolatrous greed. Our revelrous parties are not in honor of any god but in honor of our own lusts for pleasure, the worship of self and illicit sex. Remember the risks you have taken when you were outside the faith pursing your desires without restraint. Remember the consequences you have experienced? Perhaps, you escaped calamity, but remember the ones who did not escape—a childhood friend in jail for robbery, the son who died fleeing the police during a car chase drunk with alcohol, illicit sex resulting in disease and destruction of relationships.

Those outside the faith who live such lifestyles are amazed at believers who abstain. They are amazed that you no longer are living the way you used to, the way they do now, which is in reckless excess. In their amazement, they make fun of you, maligning you, actually blaspheming your name, and, thereby, also blaspheming the Lord God. They recklessly expose themselves to dangerous addictions of the flesh and of the soul, compromising their conscious decision-making, risking accidents, disease, and death. Even now, they would laugh and scoff at such words, but they will have to give an accounting of their lives. Those who treat you like this will have to give a defense to God, who is ready to judge those who are alive and those who are already dead. He is ready and prepared to judge, and they will have to discuss it with him. In light of the world's despairing condition, we who are in Christ are once again reminded of the need to pursue obedient living, resisting the temptation of former desires.

We see here in the writings of Peter that judgment will come, and it must first start with the house of God, the Church. Thankfully, the judgment that starts with the house of God is not for our condemnation but for our purification. However, on the last day, there will not be much of a discussion with these who refuse to believe, as much as there will be a giving of an account to God. From the words of Jesus, we know that these blasphemers will stand before the throne of God trying to defend their actions, and, in the end, they will be forced to depart from his presence. For our part, we would benefit from remembering that these scoffers will not answer to us but to our Father who comes to our defense. Maintaining a posture of faith and humility will bring glory to our God, not a boastful taunting of those who are lost.

Peter tells us that the dead were evangelized or given the proclamation of the work of Christ. This was done with a purpose. The purpose was that they may be judged, judged as human beings with respect to the flesh and that they may live with respect to God in or by the Spirit. Are these, who were evangelized, those who died in the flood mentioned in chapter three, or are they simply those who were evangelized when they were alive but are now dead? If the former case were so, would that not be giving them a second chance after death? Would that not be unthinkable or unacceptable if we believe that it is appointed to men once to die and then be judged? The perspective most consistent with the whole of Gospel teaching is that these who were now dead were once alive, and it was then the Gospel was preached to them. While this question may not be answered in a way that satisfies every curiosity, what can be applied from this passage?

I would emphasize that the end result of evangelization is life. We hear the Gospel, and our hearts are convicted of the sin we have lived in while in human flesh. Yet, now that we have believed this Gospel, we can live by the Spirit of God. We were dead in our sins and trespasses, but now we are alive through faith. God sends forth his truth so that we may be able to give an accurate accounting of our lives. Once confronted with the truth that can set us free, we have the opportunity to believe. One who is so enlightened can no longer say, "This is the life into which I was destined," but rather now he must say, "This is the choice I have made." May we all receive the Word of God so that life is birthed within us.

The End Is Near: Love and Serve One Another

> The end of all things is near. Therefore be sound minded and sober for the purpose of prayer. Above all things have fervent love for each other, for love hides a multitude of sins. Be hospitable to one another without complaint, just as each person has received a grace gift, for the purpose of ministering to each other as good stewards of the many faceted grace of God. If anyone speaks, it should be as messages from God. If anyone serves it should be with the strength that God supplies so that he may be glorified in all things, through Jesus Christ. To him be the glory and the power for all eternity. Amen.
>
> —1 Peter 4:7–11

Peter declares that the end of all things is near. With the resurrection of Christ, the world entered a new era, the time of the end. We are nearer to Christ's coming now than when we first believed, and we continue to look forward to his soon return. Since the end is near, we are exhorted to be of a sound and clear mind, having clarity of thought, and to be sober for the purpose of prayer. It is not difficult to become clouded in our thinking, distracted from the things that matter for eternity, and intoxicated with the desires of the flesh, hence, the exhortation to also be sober. This soberness goes far beyond avoiding chemical intoxication to having clarity of thought with the ability to see life without the obstructions and distractions of worldly appetites.

The purpose for this clarity of thought and soberness of mind is prayer. We do not want to pray our fantasies but rather pray for the will of God. For the most part, when our minds are clouded and full of the world's intoxicating distractions, we do not pray. If we do pray while under the influence of these distractions, we are hard of hearing and sluggish to the leading of the Spirit. In fact, the only thing we are likely to hear or perceive from God under these conditions is the need for our own repentance. If we find ourselves in such a condition, let us so repent, changing both our behaviors and our thought processes. Oh, we need not be fooled to think this is an easy road but rather be convinced that it is a necessary one. One of our greatest failures is that we will not pray. Our greatest successes are found through the discipline and passion of prayer. However, the act of prayer must not be mistaken as the portal of power. Rather, it is the communion of prayer, the fellowship of prayer with the living God from whom power is received.

The preceding words of Peter have exhorted us to the importance of prayer and our state of mind as we enter into it. Now, however, we are exhorted to have, as top priority, a disposition of fervent love within our midst as his church. Above and before all things, before all other spiritual activities, is the primary importance of having love. Why? Love hides and covers a multitude of sins. Proverbs states this precious principle, and the apostle James shows how to put this into action.

> Hatred stirs up strife, But love covers all sins. (Proverbs 10:12, NKJV)

> Remember this: Whoever turns a sinner from the error of their way will save them from death and cover over a multitude of sins. (James 5:20, NIV)

We must first dismiss the notion that our love conceals the sins of the disobedient. We do not aid their disobedience through a love of denial. Rather, we show love and mercy to those who sin against us so we may be reconciled together with them. Proverbs 10:12 points us to the idea of reconciliation. Our hatred will stir up strife and dissension, but love covers all transgression. Love stifles the stirring up of strife. James 5:20 further supports this idea of reconciliation. Through love we can continue to relate to our brothers who have sinned against us with mercy and forgiveness. There is no time in these last days for dissention, division, and un-forgiveness. God has given to us the ministry of reconciliation, helping the disobedient to return to God.

Love is the greatest spiritual activity we can exercise. We are reminded by the Love chapter of the Bible: "The greatest of these is love" (1 Corinthians 13). We are also reminded of the words of Jesus: "They will know you are my disciples by your love for one another." Love is the foundation for the Gospel message, the very platform from which it is preached. Our own love for one another declares the saving grace of Jesus Christ and the love that God has toward us. With this fervent, constant love in mind, we are given more specific direction on how to live out this love practically in our relationships.

Specific Ways to Live Out Love

Now with the end of all things being near and the priority of love in mind, we are to live with specific goals in focus, especially as it pertains to our relationships with others. First, we are exhorted to be hospitable to each other and to do it without complaining. *Hospitable* is a combination of two Greek words meaning "stranger" and "love," or in other words, stranger-loving. We find in Hebrews 13:2 (NKJV), "Do not forget to entertain strangers, for by so doing some have unwittingly entertained angels without knowing it." The basic idea behind the Greek word for hospitality was rooted in entertaining strangers, being kind to them. This kindness of hospitality would, of course, extend to those of our Church family. If we would show hospitality to strangers, how much more should we give it to those near to us in the family of God and, furthermore, practice such hospitality without complaining. Not only do we dispense grace to others but we also do it with grace and love.

We have each received a gift of ministry from God, and we are to serve with that gift as good stewards of God's manifold and diverse grace. May God grant us that servant heart that we may serve without complaining, doing it to the glory of God in the strength he provides. With respect to the ministering gifts God has given to us, Peter specifically exhorts that if anyone speaks in ministry it should proceed as a word from God, truly speaking his Word. If anyone serves, whatever that service be, let it be done out of the strength that God supplies. This is so that in everything God may be glorified through Jesus Christ.

All is to be done to the glory of God. It is his kingdom that is being advanced in the strength of his Spirit. All glory and power and dominion belong to God forever and ever. Amen.

Rejoice in Suffering and Commit Yourself to God

> Beloved, do not be surprised at the fiery trial you are experiencing, as though something strange were happening to you. But to the extent you are participating in the sufferings of Christ, rejoice; so that when his glory is revealed you may rejoice exuberantly! If you are insulted because of the name of Christ, you are blessed, because the Spirit of glory and of God rests upon you.
>
> —1 Peter 4:12–14

Peter encouraged his readers not to be overwhelmed but to rejoice when they experience suffering. Peter gives two major directives to those experiencing the challenges of life, two imperatives: "Do not be surprised," and "Rejoice!" Do not be surprised or amazed at the fiery ordeal you may be experiencing, as though something strange were happening to you. These events are opportunities to show the validity of your faith. The persecution experienced by Peter's audience occurred because of their adherence to faith in Jesus Christ, a faith foreign to the pagan culture that the church lived in.

Our previous acquaintances were surprised and amazed that we no longer ran around with them in their fleshly behaviors. While they are surprised at our new behavior, we are not to be surprised at their behavior toward us. This fiery trial is painful and yet a blessing. To the extent we share Christ's sufferings, persecutions for our faith in Christ, we may rejoice. We rejoice now with a purpose so that in the future we may rejoice with even greater joy when his glory is revealed. It seems from this passage that our rejoicing in this life during our trials for Christ stores up even greater joy for us for the future. If we are insulted for the name of Christ, we are blessed, for as a result the Spirit of glory and of God rests upon us. Scripture boldly testifies that you are blessed when people revile you for your faith and life in God, (Matthew 10:24–25; Luke 6:23, 40; John 13:16, 15:18–21; Isaiah 1:1–2; 2 Corinthians 3:8, 17–18).

What are the fiery ordeals we experience today? There are those that come from the hands of people, and there are those that come from the spiritual realm. There are external as well as internal fiery trials. Many fiery trials come not as a result of our witness to Christ but as a result of life itself: broken relationships, the death of a loved one, loss of a job. Many more could be enumerated. While they may not come as a result of our witness for Christ, they can be an occasion for a witness to Christ. Through our trials and tribulations, we can display faith and grace that will get the attention of a lost world, especially those outside of Christ who might be observing our lives. They will be drawn to God who gives us the victory through Christ.

There are trials we have experienced that are a direct result of our faith in Christ. It is through these that we share in his glory and in which we may greatly rejoice.

The church through the ages has experienced intense and difficult persecution to the point of painful imprisonments and difficult deaths. More than one woman has suffered abandonment and divorce because of her newfound faith. Family persecutions and ridicule are not uncommon. For the most part, experience of suffering for the faith in the United States has been mild, yet suffering throughout the world has remained harsh in many regions, resulting in prison and death. We must pray for our brothers and sisters around the world who suffer such pains. May God give them such grace to endure and so bear witness to the living Christ that their persecutors may be saved. May they endure to the end so that they also may be glorified in the day of our Lord.

Suffering in the inner life occurs throughout the world. Our struggle against the flesh, the world, and the devil is heated and necessary. Here we all share in the sufferings of our Lord as we resist sin and the devil, resisting the temptations and inner torments of the world. This life of inner suffering is reflected in Hebrews 12:4 where the author writes that his readers have not yet resisted sin to the point of shedding their own blood. This he says after chapter eleven where he lists the many saints who died for their faith and fight against sin. Our many prayers and fasting are part of this warfare, preparing us for battle in the kingdom of God, both for the outward manifestation of the kingdom in the world and the coming of the kingdom in our own hearts.

However, in the midst of this suffering, we must not lose sight of Peter's exhortation to rejoice and Jesus's example of joy-focused endurance. If we suffer for the sake of his name, we are most blessed. Remember that for the joy that was set before him, he endured.

> Looking unto Jesus, the author and finisher of our faith, who for the joy that was set before Him endured the cross, despising the shame, and has sat down at the right hand of the throne of God. (Hebrews 12:2, NKJV)

We can shout out loud in any circumstance that we are blessed, singing a song of declaration: "I am blessed, I am blessed. Every day of my life I am blessed!" I can imagine more than one person crying out, "Fantasy! No one acts like that." It may be true that few respond in this way, but the example of Christ given to us in Hebrews should encourage our troubled hearts. The example of Paul and Silas praying and singing while in prison, after having been beaten, shows us the joy that Christ brings, when we endure suffering for our faith in him (Acts 16:22–25).

Suffer for Christ, Not for Personal Crimes or Offenses

> Let no one suffer as a murderer or thief or evil doer or as one who meddles in things not his business. But if he suffers as a Christian, let him not be ashamed, but let him glorify God in this name. For it is time for judgment to begin with the house of God. And if it starts with us, what will the end be for those who do not believe the gospel that comes from God. And if the righteous are saved with difficulty (or barely),

> where shall the godless and the sinner appear?
> Therefore, those who also are suffering according
> to the will of God, should continually entrust
> their souls to the faithful creator by doing good.
>
> —1 Peter 4:15–19

Peter exhorts his readers not to let anyone among them suffer as a criminal of any degree, whether as a gross criminal such as a murderer or thief or as an evil doer of any kind, or even as one who intrudes into things that are not his business. Of course, one who commits these crimes will likely suffer the penalties, if not here, certainly in the judgment day. One must also consider the unfortunate possibility that a Christian may be found guilty of any one of these crimes. The idea here is that we must temper our own behavior so that we do not commit such offenses, for there will be suffering associated with them. We are also hereby commissioned to help others avoid such condemning behaviors that do not bring life. Rather, we have the opportunity to provide an environment of service and accountability that will train them for godly citizenship.

While the idea of avoiding suffering for crimes committed through disobedience is motivating, avoiding suffering is not the goal of this exhortation. Peter's point is, if we are to suffer for anything let it be for being a Christian. If this kind of suffering occurs, let us not be ashamed. Shame will move one to avoid being identified with Christ. Rather, let us glorify God by the name of Christ and endure unjust suffering for his name confidently and with joyful satisfaction. Remember, you are not alone; Christ has preceded you on this journey and is with you now strengthening and comforting.

Peter says it is time for judgment to begin at the house of God. Today, this passage is quoted and referred to as if this were a new thing. If it was time for judgment to begin with the house of God in Peter's day, what is it now? We are people of covenant, children of God, yet God is going to take inventory of his people. God purges his people as needed. In fact, God continually assesses and evaluates the condition of his people and disciplines them because they are his children whom he loves.

While God's judgment begins with us, it will not end with us. This prompts the question of what will the end be for those who disobey the Gospel of God? If it is with difficulty that the righteous are saved, where shall the ungodly and sinner appear? Where will they be found? What will happen to them? The answer to this is simple, although not directly answered here. The question itself is just a way for Peter to remind us of the plight of those who persist in their rebellion against God and refuse to believe in the Lord Jesus Christ. They will find themselves outside the presence of God and his glorious light.

Let us reflect a moment on Peter's words: "And if the righteous are saved with difficulty (or barely)"[9]. How is it that the righteous are barely saved or saved with difficulty? Peter does not elaborate on this; how can we? However, a New Testament passage where Jesus said it would be easier for a camel to go through the eye of a needle than

---

9. This is a reference to Proverbs 11:31, a direct quote from the Septuagint (the Greek translation of the Hebrew Scriptures).

for a rich man to enter the kingdom of God comes to mind. The disciples were exasperated and responded to Jesus, saying, "Who then could be saved?" Jesus replied to them, saying that this was impossible with men but that with God all things were possible. Salvation is a human impossibility. We cannot save ourselves. In fact, we are doomed for sure if we try to save ourselves rather than look to Christ. His sacrifice and atonement paid the price for mankind's rebellions, no ifs ands or buts! There is only one way, and it's Jesus.

Therefore, with these ideas in mind, as we suffer according to the will of God, let us entrust ourselves to our faithful creator. The entire passage of verse nineteen has our behavior in focus. It is by continually doing good that we entrust ourselves to God. In the face of suffering, in the face of temptations, we can put ourselves in God's faithful hands by our obedience to him. Let us not become weary in doing well, and let us not retaliate against our persecutors. As Jesus has said: "Do good to those who hate you" (Luke 6:27, NIV). It is by the actions of our faith that we entrust our lives to God.

Chapter 5

Peter Gives Words of Wisdom to Church Leaders

> Therefore, I beseech the elders among you, I who am a fellow elder and witness of the sufferings of Christ and fellow partaker of the glory about to be revealed.
>
> —1 Peter 5:1

Peter: A Fellow Elder and Governance of the Church

The exhortation given here is now directed to the elders/leaders of the churches. Remember that Peter is addressing more than one church and, hence, more than one elder. However, some church government structures have been built upon the idea of multiple elders working together in one church. Multiple eldership congregations could very well be likely.

It appears that the position of elder was carried over from Jewish leadership. We see in the New Testament the elders with the Pharisees and the teachers of the Law joined together against Jesus and the apostles (Matthew 15:2; Acts 4:5). The elders as a ruling group of Israel can even be found during the intertestamental period, the time between the Old and New Testaments (1 Maccabees 7:33). The book of Ezra written at the very end of the Old Testament era also refers to elders as leaders of the people. Both the prophets and the writings of the Old Testament refer to elders. The concept of elders in the New Testament and here in 1 Peter is not new, but the contemporary way the synagogue and the church were then governed.

The book of Acts gives historical context to the leadership of elders in the church. Paul and Barnabas carried gifts to Judea to provide relief from an impending famine. These gifts were to be given to the elders of the church for distribution (Acts 11:30). Acts 14:23 describes Paul and Barnabas appointing elders in each of the churches they established. Acts 15:2–4 shows that both apostles and elders represented a governing board in Jerusalem and that they were each a group to themselves, yet they worked together to address problems in the church.

Elder in the Greek New Testament is *presbuteros*. It is the word presbyter used today. Typically, a presbyter is one who is a leader of pastors over particular geographical areas in certain denominations. But Peter refers to himself here as a fellow elder in this epistle, placing himself at the same level as all other elders, not above them. It is his apostleship that elevates his authority above other elders.

There are a variety of church governments today. Represented are single elderships, board of elders, and congregationally run democratic structures. The day-to-day management decisions have been overseen by a great many government structures, but ultimately there is the head pastor who is responsible as a spiritual shepherd. His staff assists him and serves the church, but he is responsible both to God and to the church as its spiritual leader. While some church governmental structures may not use the term *elders* to describe its leaders, functionally we have elders in church bodies today as pastors and key lay leaders. We may apply these exhortations to the local church in this way.

At the beginning of this epistle, Peter asserts his apostolic authority. He elaborates on his qualifications or, rather, his position of authority to make this exhortation. He is a leader of leaders. Yet, he is also a fellow elder and witness of the sufferings of Christ and one who will share in the glory that is about to be revealed. Although he is more than their equal in his calling and apostolic ministry, he presents himself as a colleague. We can learn from Peter that whatever our position of leadership responsibility in the church is, we are to have a disposition of humility and grace that counteracts the temptation to pompous pride.

One additional point about Peter's self-description is noteworthy. He is one who will share in the glory that is about to be revealed. Thankfully, this glory is one that all of us who are in Christ will share when he returns.

Pastoral Responsibilities

> Shepherd the flock of God in your midst,
> overseeing not under compulsion but willingly,
> according to the will of God, and not greedily
> but freely, and not as lording over those entrusted
> to you but being examples of the flock.
>
> —1 Peter 5:2–3

While this specific word is given to the church leadership, it has applications for all of us to follow. Many of the teachings Peter gives apply to every member of the church, others apply to those specifically mentioned—husbands, wives, children, and here pastors or elders-shepherds—but we can all learn some general principles from them as well.

Elders are to shepherd the flock of God that is under their care. Each presbyter, elder, or pastor has the responsibility and privilege of serving and caring for the members of their church. As a church grows large, one man cannot service every individual. Structures need to be established to provide personal pastoral care through other leaders. This is often accomplished through small group fellowships where individual discipleship and development of ministry gifts can take place. As the church grows and increases, so the pastoral staff must also increase and the people be mobilized to more diligent and expanded areas of service. This is a more sure way to shepherd a larger group of people.

Each elder is reminded that the flock which they oversee is not theirs but rather belongs to God. We all answer to the Lord as well as to each other. Discussions with staff members over church policy issues are appropriate at times, but we must trust God's leadership. Both pastor and congregation are to remember that Christ our Lord has been appointed by the Father to be head over everything for the church. If more people would pray to Jesus to direct the leadership of the church rather than murmur their complaints or push mutinous petitions, the will of God would flourish among us. Petition the Lord with your concerns instead. I have witnessed policy changes in churches as a direct result of prayer. Trust the headship of Christ over the church.

Elders shepherd the flock by overseeing it willingly not because they have to under some kind of compulsion. What might compel someone to serve as a pastor over a church? Is this an inner compulsion or an outward force pressing him into service? It seems that the latter is the case discussed in this passage, since pastors are exhorted to serve willingly and to do so with respect to their relationship with God within the bounds of his will. Such a ministry should be engaged in as a result of God's leading, not from the pressures of men. Children have been pushed into careers chosen by their parents, but children must be taught to discover the will of God for themselves. Gifted individuals may be pleaded with to pastor a church, but it is the will of God that must be followed. Shepherding must be done from the proper motives of inner desire and God-directed passion. It is not out of greed for money or fame that they serve but out of motivation from godly desires within, eagerly, willingly, and readily serving the church.

Elders and shepherds are not to lord over those given to their care, but they are to be examples to the flock, showing them not only in word but also in deed how it is to be in the will of God. This is where a pastor can rise or fall. Is he the servant of all, or the one whom all are to serve? A harsh taskmaster for a pastor does not reflect the glorious grace of God. Remember, the Lord said that "the greatest among you shall be your servant." While Jesus led with authority, he did so with love and service. He did not come to be served but to serve and to give his life.

The elder is an example for the flock. Observe your pastor's life and learn from him. Of course, he is not perfect, don't expect him to be. But learn the godly disciplines from your pastors: prayer, worship, Bible truth, evangelism, giving. Learn more than information; learn character, godliness, and passion. Furthermore, pastors, train and disciple your members. Show them, train them, and observe them so they may be equipped to disciple others.

Pastoral Reward

> And when the Chief Shepherd appears, you will receive the unfading crown of glory.
>
> —1 Peter 5:4

Elders and shepherds, by executing their duties as prescribed, will receive the unfading crown of glory as a reward when the Chief Shepherd—our Lord Jesus

Christ—appears. Once again, our sites are directed toward the future coming and appearance of Jesus. This is when we will all receive the fullness of our rewards. There shall be incorruptible crowns of life and of righteousness given to all who believe in the Lord Christ. However, in the New Testament, this unfading crown of glory is reserved for those who shepherd the flock of God. Nowhere else in Scripture is this crown of glory mentioned.

While this may not be a literal crown, the glory to be seen is real. It is enriching to know the love of God as it is expressed in his desire to glorify his servants, sons, and daughters. As our servants of the church do not seek their own glory but seek to glorify God and serve his people, they will subsequently be glorified by the one whom they glorify.

Responsibilities of the Church: Humility, Trust, and Self-Control

> Likewise, young men, submit to elders. And everyone clothe yourselves with humility, for God opposes proud people but he gives grace to those who are humble. Therefore, humble yourselves under the mighty hand of God, so that he may lift you up when the time is right, casting all your anxiety upon him because he cares for you.
>
> —1 Peter 5:5–7

As Peter had a word for the elders of the church, he also had a specific message for its younger members under their authority. They are to submit to the elders who govern, honoring their decisions and giving respect to their leadership. Relationships in the church are various and multifaceted. It matters to God how his children relate to each other. The younger generation will be given opportunity and training for ministry. This is designed to be done by the older and more experienced members of the church.

Peter expands his earlier exhortation to be humble by exhorting everyone to clothe themselves with humility toward one another (1 Peter 3:8). Why? Because God is against the proud but gives grace to those who are humble. Pride exemplifies self-sufficiency rather than God-sufficiency and attempts to bring glory to self rather than glory to God. Pride also seeks its own needs most often at the expense of the needs of others. This godly character of humility is described as a garment to be put on. Our will is involved and required. Never mistake humility for weakness or timidity; rather, it is the graciousness of controlled strength. This is not a mere outward appearance of humility but an internal character displayed through visible behavior. Humility is an internal disposition of greatness in the kingdom of God (Matthew 18:1–4).

There are over one hundred references to *pride* or *proud* in the Scriptures, and in them we find there is no blessing in having a proud haughty heart. Peter's warning is that such a person finds opposition from God. But the good news is that he gives grace to the humble and keeps on giving it. The proud can have a change of heart by listening and obeying the warnings given.

There is blessing in humility. Moses was acclaimed to be the most humble man on earth (Numbers 12:3). Regardless of his high position, Moses maintained a heart of humbleness before God and before the people. God saves the humble (2 Samuel 22:28). In this passage, it appears that Peter is specifically expounding on Proverbs 3:34 (LXX): "The Lord opposes the proud but gives grace to the humble."

Humility is a disposition we may have toward one another, but it is also one that we have with respect to our relationship with God. We humble ourselves under his mighty hand. This is something *we* are to do, for it is our responsibility to submit ourselves under his authority and power. We are aware of the awesomeness of our great God who has created the universe and everything that exists. We bow before him in humble worship. Furthermore, we are given both the purpose and result of our response of humility to God: that he may lift us up.

The result is that God will lift us up at the right time when he appears in the last day. We have experienced in this life from time to time the lifting up of the Lord in our own lives with specific moments and cases we can recall. However, this is not what is being referred to here. Our lifting up in the last day is our resurrection and exaltation by the Lord himself, a sharing in his great glory. The glory we receive in this life is only a glimpse of the glory to come. The more we know God in personal fellowship, the easier it is to joyfully humble ourselves before him with faith and confidence. When we come to know him, we humbly submit out of love and gratitude, being thankful for all his blessings.

Part of humbling ourselves before God is that of casting all our cares and worries upon him. This is an act of confidence and faith, an acknowledgement of his ability and benevolence, his power and his love. The question is: Why would God want us to cast our anxieties and concerns upon him? The question is explicitly and directly answered for us: Because our lives matter to him. God forever loves us! This fact has been the subject of wonder and amazement. Both Job and David have pondered the care and concern God has for us.

> What is man, that You should exalt him, That You should set Your heart on him…? (Job 7:17, NKJV)

> What is man that You are mindful of him, And the son of man that You visit him? (Psalm 8:4, NKJV)

> LORD, what is man, that You take knowledge of him? Or the son of man, that You are mindful of him? (Psalm 144:3, NKJV)

Nothing is too great and nothing too small for God to concern himself over our lives. He chooses to be intimately aware and active. Sometimes, we are acutely aware of his presence; sometimes, we must infer it from his great and precious promises. Either way, the reality of his presence is with us. It would benefit us to listen astutely for the inner voice of God's Spirit who will lead us by his caring love. Listen in prayer and in the study of his Word, listen in praise and worship, and listen to the voice of his creative power that simply speaks through creation with resounding complexity. The great expanse of creation displays his care and mindfulness of us, we who are but a minute part of it all. Are these not reasons enough to cast all our cares on him with all faith and humility?

Victory Over the Enemy of Our Souls

> Be sober, watchful and alert. Your adversary the devil is walking about like a roaring lion actively seeking someone to swallow or gulp down. Resist him by being steadfast in the faith, knowing that the same sufferings are being endured by your brothers throughout the world.
>
> —1 Peter 5:8–9

Once again, Peter exhorts us to be sober, as he did in chapter four, verse seven, and to be watchful and on guard. His repeated exhortation reminds us and indicates to us the importance of sobriety and alertness and that our mental sobriety is often challenged. We have an adversary—the devil—and he is walking about like a roaring lion on the prowl, actively seeking someone to gulp down and swallow whole. This imagery is meant to get our attention, to help wake us up into sobriety and watchfulness. Who wants that to be their end? The devil is a predator looking to create havoc in the world and destroy lives. Remember the warning of Jesus that the thief comes to steal to kill and to destroy (John 10:10).

Praise God, however, that Jesus has come so that we might have abundant life. This life is extended to us in many ways, even making us aware of the devil's schemes so that we may avoid and be rescued from his works.

Remember the warning given to Cain, "Sin is crouching at your door" (Genesis 4:7, NIV). Sin was described to Cain as a predator waiting to attack him. This description is also meant to benefit us so that we too may be warned. But thanks to God for the victory that is ours in Christ, and this victory comes to us with soberness and watchfulness. This watchfulness is not only for our own sakes but so that we can be agents of deliverance, helping others who may be unaware. We seek not only our own good but also the good of others. "Rescue the perishing care for the dying."

We are in warfare against this enemy. Our warfare has two basic components to it—internal and external. We battle against the lust of the flesh so we are not being led away by our own desires, and we also battle against the world and the devil. The external battle takes prominence in this passage, characterized by the sufferings caused by human oppression and persecution. However, even the external sufferings of persecutions experienced may exert internal pressure to compromise and hopelessness.

We are to resist by standing against this predator firmly in faith. Some English translations have "the faith" as part of their rendering of the Greek New Testament, while others have "your faith." This is not a textual variant but a difference in translation, one emphasizing the facts of the Christian faith and the other emphasizing personal trust in God. Commentaries have not proven to be conclusive in defining more precisely what is meant by faith here; both perspectives are found in various commentaries. However, an answer is not beyond grasp. Are we to understand faith in this context as the substance of what we believe as Christian doctrine, or is it faith as in whom we believe describing faith as a personal relationship of trust? Is faith defined here as what we believe, or in whom we believe? While other books of the Bible often talk about the battle for believing specific truths of the faith, faith here is connected to the endurance of suffering for being Christian. This would indicate that the believer is being encouraged to resist the devil by being firm in his own personal faith, his relationship of trust with God. We are reminded of the exhortation of the apostle Paul to take up the shield of faith with which we can defend against the enemy's attacks. The letter of 1 John assures of victory over the world. "For everyone born of God overcomes the world. This is the victory that has overcome the world, even our faith" (1 John 5:4, NIV).

Furthermore, we resist the oppressor with the knowledge that the family of God throughout the world is also experiencing the same sufferings we are experiencing. Knowing that we are not alone in our persecutions can be a great encouragement for us, whether as individuals or the church or as the body of Christ. Peter reminds his readers that throughout the world the *brothers* (a more personalized and endearing term) are enduring the same sufferings. Keep this fact in mind for your personal encouragement and for their prayerful support.

When the enemy attacks, do not remain isolated, believing the fantasy that you are the only one suffering as you are. Like Paul, we endure sharing in the sufferings of Christ as indicated in the following passages.

> I want to know Christ—yes, to know the power of his resurrection and participation in his sufferings, becoming like him in his death. (Philippians 3:10, NIV)
>
> And our hope for you is firm, because we know that just as you share in our sufferings, so also you share in our comfort. (2 Corinthians 1:7, NIV)

It would serve us well to be more aware of the trials our brothers and sisters in the faith are experiencing throughout the world and not hide from them in ignorance. They are an encouragement for us, and we are for them.

The Stabilizing Grace of God

> And the God of all grace, who called you into his eternal glory, in Christ Jesus, after you have suffered a little while, himself shall restore, stabilize, strengthen and establish you. To him be the power forever. Amen.
>
> —1 Peter 5:10–11

Beginning with verse ten, Peter gives his closing blessings and greetings. Once again, these blessings and greetings are packed with anointed truths; they are more than parting thoughts. Peter elaborates on God, who blesses us. He is the God of all grace, and he imparts all his grace to us freely and liberally. This grace has great effect in our lives. By it, he brings salvation to us and works his sanctification in us by this same grace. "For the grace of God that brings salvation has appeared to all men" (Titus

2:11, NKJV), and it is the grace of God that teaches us to say no to ungodliness and worldly passions (Titus 2:12). He is the one who called us into his eternal glory through Christ Jesus by sending his only begotten Son to pay the price for our redemption; he bids us to *come*.

Though sufferings will come for a little while, after our brief sufferings, God will restore us and repair any and all brokenness in our lives. Furthermore, he will stabilize, strengthen, and establish us so that we will be healed, made whole, and empowered by his Spirit. In response to God's work of repair and strengthening, we give thankful praise. To him be the power and strength forever. Amen!

Final Greetings

> Through Silas, whom I consider a faithful brother, I have written briefly to you, encouraging and bearing witness that this is the true grace of God, in which you stand. The church in Babylon, chosen together with you, greets you and so does my son Mark. Greet one another with a kiss of love. Peace to all who are in Christ.
>
> —1 Peter 5:12–14

Peter acknowledges his associate Silas, giving him deserved praise for his faithfulness and help in writing this epistle. As a result of Peter's association with Silas, he was able to determine this brother's faithfulness. It was not simply from reports of others, but it was his personal interaction that brought this determination. Note that this is also one of Paul's devoted associates. May we be like Silas and gain a good reputation of faithfulness from our work, so that those who know us in the faith may also recognize our faithfulness and be encouraged. This will increase the fruit of our labors for God's glory, as we are recommended to the service of others.

Peter characterizes his letter as a brief writing in which he has sought to exhort and give witness to them. What has been written declares the true grace of God. Our understanding of grace must be obtained from that which has been written, for that is how God has revealed himself to us—through the writings of his servants. We want God's true grace, not something that falls short of it, not some synthetic substitute. Now that this grace has been declared and revealed to us, we may stand firm in it and be strengthened by it. Is this not your desire?

The church in Rome (called Babylon for its location in Rome's immoral capital) from where Peter wrote this epistle sent greetings to the churches. These Roman Christians were called to Christ, together with his readers to form one people. Mark, an apparent disciple of Peter and another one of Paul's late associates, greets them as well.

The point of application we can make here is that we are to have genuine care for others, not just those of our own fellowship or church but also for those outside our own circles of associations. We must also say that our fellowship extends beyond our own denominational constructs and ideologies that separate us from faithful fellowship with other Christians. We are one body with one Lord, comprised of many servants, with whom we are bound together under the Lordship of Christ and Fatherhood of God.

After greetings were given from the church at Rome, greetings were to be given within the church to one another with a kiss of love. Let us have genuine pure affection for each other, for we are family and members of each other. While not every culture shows affection and friendship with a kiss (though some still do today), we can, at least, show the affection that is appropriate for our day. Friendly handshakes and hugs are among the most common greetings, and sometimes a hand on the shoulder or pat on the back. In any case, appropriate physical contact can be made as a way of affirming love for one another and as a way of passing on the blessings of God.

Peace, shalom, be to those who are in Christ. The final blessing of God's peace is pronounced. The blessing of God's wholeness is found in Christ alone. He is the means by which the Father has passed on to us all the blessings of heaven. Through his abiding covenant, eternal peace and wholeness have come to us, not just to a few but to all who are in Christ. Again, we see the universal blessings of God passed on to the whole church, his entire body. It is in Christ that we find the unity of faith and the wholeness of soul that overcomes every form of suffering we may experience. He himself is our peace!

Bibliography

Brenton, Lancelot Charles Lee. *The Septuagint with Apocrypha: Greek and English.* Massachusetts: Hendrickson Publishers, 1990.

Clowney, Edmund P. *The Message of 1 Peter: The Way of the Cross.* The Bible Speaks Today. Leicester, England: Inter-Varsity Press, 1988.

Michaels, J. Ramsey. *1 Peter.* Edited by David Hubbard, Glenn Barker, and Ralph Martin. Vol. 49. Word Biblical Commentary. Nashville: Thomas Nelson, 1988.

Wallace, Daniel B. *Greek Grammar beyond the Basics: An Exegetical Syntax of the New Testament.* Grand Rapids: Zondervan, 1996.